Heidelberg

English · Français · Español

Kunstverlag Edm. von König, Heidelberg/Dielheim

eccar *Fluvius.*

The last rays of the sun cast a spell over the castle.

Les derniers rayons de soleil jettent un voile.

Los últimos rayos de sol encantan el castillo.

View from Philosopher's Way over Castle Town. ▷

Vue du chemin des Philosophes sur la ville et le Vieux Pont et sur le château. Au fond, le Königstuhl (568 m).

Vista desde el «Philosophenweg» (Camino de los Filósofos).

Early History

The area around the lower Neckar was inhabited by man even in pre-historic times. The oldest human remains, that of the lower jaw of «Homo Heidelbergensis», reckoned to be some 550,000 years old, was found by workmen in 1907 in a sand pit near Mauer, a village about 15 kilometres from Heidelberg. From about 500 B.C., Celts occupied the present city area. They erected a fortress on the twin summits of the Heiligenberg against the oncoming Teutons and to which they finally retreated.

By the time Caesar's troops appeared in the area, the Celts had already been driven out by the Teutons and had wandered southwards. Sometime in the early part of the 1st century, the Romans built a bridge over the Neckar not far from the old settlement at Bergheim. This they fortified with a bastion on the right bank of the river.

Heidelberg makes its appearance in history

In the year 1155, Emperor Friedrich I, «Barbarossa», bestowed upon his half brother, Konrad von Hohenstein, the honourable title of «Pfalzgrafen bei Rhein» (Duke of the Rhine Palatinate). Emperor Friedrich II von Hohenstein in his turn bestowed upon the Wittelsbach Duke Ludwig I of Bavaria in the year 1214 the dukedom of Pfalz which remained in his family until the dissolution of the Kurpfalz in 1803.

The name «Heidelberch» appears for the first time in the year 1196 in a document belonging to the monastery at Schönau. In 1225, Ludwig I (1214–28) received a castle stronghold in Heidelberg as fief. Also in the year 1294, a castle is mentioned in documents and in 1303, there are indeed two castles mentioned for the first time. The lower stronghold, on the Jettenbühl, formed the original on which the castle ruins stand today, the upper was situated on the Little Gaisberg (Kleiner Gaisberg) at the place where the «Molkenkur» stands today. The upper fortifications were completely destroyed on 25th April, 1537, when lightning struck the powder reserves and exploded the main part of the castle.

In the 1329, the inherited lands of the Palatinate were separated from Bavaria in the Domiciliary Contract of Pavia (Hausvertrag von Pavia).

The Kurpfalz as the first power in the Empire

During his long reign (1329–90), Ruprecht I was able to promote the Kurpfalz in terms of power and standing to one of the primary forces in the Empire. When at the Reichstags (Imperial Parliaments) of Nürnberg and Metz in 1356 the Imperial Constitution of Emperor Karl IV, named the Golden Bull, finally confirmed the seven Palatinate princes as electors of German kings, Ruprecht, too, received the electoral dignity and the office of Lord High Steward (Master of the Imperial Kitchen, the most influential of court dignitaries) both for himself and for his successors as their indivisible property. A few years before his death he founded the University of Heidelberg in 1386. By the time his grandson, Ruprecht III, (1398–1410), had hardly been crowned (1401), the narrow castle could no more fulfil the demands made of it as such an important residence, and it is from this time that the simple Gothic, Ruprecht building came into existence.

One of the most popular Palatinate princes was Friedrich I, the Victorious, alluded to in the popular tongue as the «Palatinate Fritz» (Pfälzer Fritz). His reign is marked by a number of warring disputes (1449–76). Apart from a number of successful feuds, he was victorious in the important Battle of Pfeddersheim (1460) and at Seckenheim (1462) which brought upon him the reputation of being the greatest fighting hero of his time.

Ludwig V (1508–1544) fought the war of succession as to who should follow Emperor Maximilian on the side of the Habsburgs and brought it to a successful conclusion. The feud with the Sickingers and successes in the Peasants War (1525) earned the House of Kurfürsten considerable esteem. Subsequently, Ludwig became very active in introducing building operations at his residential castle. The first thing he did was to strengthen the fortifications by building new ones and by extending towers and walls. The living quarters as well as the buildings housing material and provisions around the castle courtyard were commissioned for improvement or rebuilding.

The Hall of Mirrors Building came into being in the reign of Friedrich II (1544–1556). In building it he introduced the Renaissance to the Kurfürsten castle. Up to the time he took office in Heidelberg, Friedrich's nephew, Ottheinrich, (1556–1559) had ruled over his small dukedom, Pfalz-Neuberg. By erecting the courtyard facade which was named the Ottheinrich building after him, he at the same time established a precedence in the art of German Renaissance building.

Johann Kasimir (1583–1592), Duke of the Palatinate, although he built a barrel-shaped building over the North Dungeon, he nevertheless in addition to this placed the Große Batterie towards the castle's northern flank as a protruding, defensive position.

Under his nephew, Friedrich IV, the Palatinate became the leading force in the Protestant cause in Germany. In the castle courtyard, at the same time as the Friedrichsbau was built, a counterpart was erected which was also successful like that of the Ottheinrich Building and which was just as costly if not quite as artistic as the earlier building. Despite that, however, together with the Great Altan, and especially the outer facade of the Friedrich Building, he nevertheless succeeded in producing a fine stylistic composition enhancing the mighty frontage of the castle as seen from the valley.

The Decline of the Pfalz

His son, Friedrich V (1610–1620), ascended the Palatine throne as a youth. On the northern rampart he commissioned a simple building to be erected to serve as living quarters, the English Building. The main attention of his building activities, however, was centred on the castle garden. He availed himself of the services of the famous landscape gardener, Salomon de Caus, to transform the slopes to the north and east around the castle into terraced gardens typical of that period. When, in 1619, he was elected King of Bohemia, the Thirty Years War finally broke out in all its fury. Already in November of the following year, Friedrich lost in the decisive Battle of the White Mountain both his newly acquired title of King and also his electoral dignity, fell into contempt and fled to Holland. Nothing remained to him but the title of «Winterkönig» (King-for-a-Winter) and he went down in history as such.

General Tilly, Supreme Commander of the Imperial Army, commenced on 26th August, 1622, to bombard the castle and the city, conquering the latter by storm on the 16th September. A few days later, the defenders of the castle capitulated. For the first time, the residence of the Palatine princes found itself in the hands of foreign troops.

Building activities at the castle had, since the beginning of the Thirty Years War, limited themselves to damaged buildings and the «English Building» remained to this day the last section to be erected as a living area. After Friedrich V had lost the county and the electoral dignity, both these fell in the first place to the Bavarian Wittelsbach family. At the Peace of Westfalia, Friedrich's son, Karl Ludwig, (1649–1680), at least received his inherited lands again. Patiently, and with circumspection, Karl Ludwig went about the job of building up his country again as well as attending to the damage at his family castle after the ravages of this appalling war. His only son, Karl II, (1680–1685) made it his business to strengthen the castle's defensive resources. On his death and the extinction of the line of Pfalz-Simmern, misfortune descended again and with even greater force upon the Pfalz. Karl's sister, Elisabeth Charlotte, referred to as Liselotte of the Pfalz, was married to the Duke of Orleans, brother of Louis XIV of France. He, the «Sun King», demanded the handing over of a great part of the Palatinate, this however in the name of his wife, but without her permission and contrary to the laws governing the heritage. In October, 1688, his troops marched into Heidelberg. As the armies of the allied princes, now united against the French, came manacingly near, the French withdrew under their commander Mélac in March 1689, not, however, before they had been obedient to their mandatory orders and destroyed all fortifications and ravaged the Pfalz together with its capital.

In the meantime Johann Wilhelm (1690–1716) had become Prince of the Palatine and he urged the people to re-establish the fortifications as soon as possible, and so it was that in 1691 and 1692 French troops could be repulsed from the city walls. In May, 1693, however, Heidelberg was once more in the hands of foreign forces and a few hours after its possession it became a sea of fire. Hordes of soldiers plundered the city, senselessly broke open the graves in the Church of the Holy Ghost (Heiliggeistkirche), smashing the beautifully wrought gravestones, tore the bones of the Palatine princes from their resting place and threw them into the street, taking the tin coffins in which they were housed as loot. In the castle itself they went to considerable trouble to blow up those fortifications which had escaped destruction in 1689. They plundered the palaces, looted or utterly destroyed the art treasures there as well as provisions and, with the help of pitch rings, set these on fire. Only gradually did the Heidelberg citizenry return to their wasted city after the withdrawal of the French and begin to rebuild their homes from the foundations of the old ones.

Karl Philipp (1716–1742), soon after his assumption to power, quickly began to make the palaces habitable once more. In 1718, he left Düsseldorf to take up residence in Heidelberg. His plans for a thoroughgoing reconstruction of the castle which were to take in a new, extended tract of land to the west and a wider access road were at first dashed by lack of money and finally by the wrangling of the Protestant community about the use of the Heiliggeistkirche. In 1720, he removed his residence to Mannheim where he built himself an extensive palace.

A last attempt to make Heidelberg Castle into a worthy seat of residence was undertaken by the Palatine prince, Karl Theodor, (1742–1799). When, however, during the restorations on the 24th of June, 1764, two shafts of lightning, one after the other, shattered the glass section of the hall building, setting this and the neighbouring palaces on fire once more, the prince took this as a heavenly warning and ordered that the work be stopped. Heidelberg Castle thus fell into a lifeless ruin. With the death of Karl Theodor and the extinction of the last of the older Kurpfalz line and after 470 years of independence, the Palatine was again united with Bavaria in the year 1799. The Imperial Deputation's main decision in 1803 finally sealed the fate of the Kurpfalz. Those lands to the left of the Rhine were to be given over to France, while those in part on the right to Hessen-Darmstadt; the larger area here, including Heidelberg, to Baden.

The Palaces and Domestic Buildings of the Kurfürst Castle

The oldest preserved building of the castle precincts is the simple Ruprechts Building opposite the ticket office. This almost completely undecorated Gothic palace came into being under Kurfürst Ruprecht III, who, as Ruprecht I of the Palatine, reigned as a German king from 1400–1410. The imperial eagle to the left of the entrance testifies to the fact that the commissioner of the building was of royal blood. In its talons the bird holds the beatifully wrought coat of arms of the house of Wittelsbach, the Palatine lion and the Bavarian lozenges.

There is masterly piece of sculpture appearing as the cornerstone over the entrance portraying two angels with a wreath of roses and within this a circle. Opposite and set back from its adjoining buildings, the library is the oldest building which was to break through the earlier fortified ring construction of the castle. A fine Gothic bay window decorates the facade on the first storey. At the same level, too, the adjoining Women's Room Building (Frauenzimmerbau) came into being of which only the ground floor remains today. The King's Hall, however, offers seating accomodation for 700 guests in which festivals and theatre performances take place. The splendid Renaissance palace opposite the Gate Tower bears the name of its builder, Friedrich, (1592–1610). The monumental statues of the knights on the courtyard facade and hewn from yellow sandstone represent ancestors of the Kurfürst. The upper row from the left portrays the forbears of Charles the Great, Otto von Wittelsbach, Ludwig II and Rudolf I; the next row the Emperors and kings of the Wittelsbach dynasty: Ludwig the Bavarian, Ruprecht von der Pfalz, Otto of Hungary and Christof of Denmark. The most important Palatinate princes of the old Kur line are Ruprecht I, Friedrich the Victorious and the builders of the adjoining Renaissance palaces, Friedrich II and Ottheinrich appear in the window niches of the upper storeys. The princes of the Pfalz-Simmern line are finally represented between the windows of the Castle Chapel. These are: Friedrich III, Ludwig IV, Johann Kasimir and the builder himself, Friedrich IV. The upper storeys of the Friedrich Building served the Palatine princes as a residential palace. They were restored some time before 1900 under the direction of Prof. Karl Schäfer and since then have been able once more to offer an impressive picture of solid, residential comfort enjoyed during the Renaissance period.

The Hall of Mirrors Building between the two, earlier, famous facades of the Friedrich and Ottheinrich Building which is decorated with figures, brought the first elements of the Renaissance into the residence of the Kurfürst princes around 1545. Its name can be traced to the banqueting hall on the first floor which at one time was furnished with Venetian mirrors all round the walls. The central tympanum between the arcades carries the coat of arms of Friedrich II, its builder, depicting the Palatine lions, the Bavarian lozenges and, in the third tympanum, the imperial orb which Friedrich received from Emperor Karl V in 1544 as the mark of honour of an

Imperial Lord High Steward. The facade of the Ottheinrich Building, constructed as it is from many elements harmoniously brought together, knows no rival north of the Alps. The artistically decorated cornice work and the varied decoration of the half columns divide the frontage into uniformly composed areas whereby each double window is separated from its neighbour by a figure housed within a niche. The richly decorated portal integrated above a flight of steps resembles a triumphal arch and bears a medallion in which the likeness of Ottheinrich is to be found, together with his coat of arms and an inscription. The windows, which are in the form of a cross on the ground floor, are crowned by triangular gables in which Roman coins from the collection of the art-obsessed builders are depicted. Next to the Atlas figures of the portal, we can recognise at the bottom, left: Joshua, Samson, Hercules and David – the heroes of the Old Testament. The figures on the first storey symbolize five of the most important virtues: Strength (with the broken column), Faith (with the Bible), Love and Motherliness (with children), Hope (with an anchor) and Justice (with scales and sword). The seven figures in the upper portion represent the gods of Roman antiquity which have been arranged around the sun and moon as well as the five great planets, Saturn, Mars, Venus, Mercury and Luna and above these, at one time in front of the two gables, Sol and Jupiter.

On the ground floor of the Ottheinrich Building and next to the Ludwig Building and the Apothekerturm (Apothecary's Tower), the German Pharmaceutical Museum has now found permanent location.

The coat of arms bearing the date 1524 on the centre stair tower is that of Ludwig V, the castle's great founder. The wing to the south of the residential palace once housed the steward's buildings, the Brunnenhalle (Well House) and the Soldiers' Building, today's ticket office.

Some distance away from the castle courtyard and adjacent to the viewing terrace and the Great Altan, Johann Kasimir's (1583–1592) narrow Wine Vat Building stands and together with the Little Altan above, completes the row. Today, it houses Karl Theodor's huge wine vat with a capacity of 221,726 litres, the largest fillable wine barrel in the world. A hundred and thirty oak trees were needed to build this vessel which has a diameter of 7 metres and which is 8.50 metres long. Its only decoration is the large coat of arms carrying the initials of Karl Theodor. To the left of the pair of compasses and the plane which were used during the construction of the vat, one can still see a section of the wine conduit which, via a pump device, linked the vat to the banqueting hall, that is, the King's Hall. The small statue is that of the dwarf, Perkeo, court fool and guardian of the vat under Karl-Philipp and Karl-Theodor. According to legend, he died after he had been persuaded to drink a glass of water instead of his accustomed wine. He still remains the symbolic figure of Heidelberg's Fastnacht. Again, according to legend, the imprint of a boot to be found in one of the sandstone slabs on the Great Altan is that of a scorned knight who, in full armour, is said to have jumped from the window of his lady love's room in the top storey of the Friedrich Building.

The Fortifications of the Castle of Heidelberg

The least danger of attack was to the north and west, since here the steep slopes offered natural protection. However, it is here that we find the strongest tower with a diameter of 30 metres situated just on the northeastern corner and called the Thick Tower. After being blown up there remained only the shell-half towards the slope side conveying an impressive idea of the defensive strength of these fortifications whose walls were 7 metres thick all the way round. In the 17th century, Friedrich V commissioned the original timbered upper storey to be dismantled, and to provide more space, he set up in its place a thin-walled, sixteen-sided banqueting hall and theatre fitted with large windows. In so doing, he thus provided a ballroom with a surface area of over 500 square metres immediately adjacent to his palace, the English Building.

The north-eastern corner tower, the Bell Tower, was originally a defensive construction one storey high. In the course of time, however, several storeys were added to it to serve as living quarters.

The Great Battery was placed in front of the Altan and served as an arsenal. Kurfürst Karl had the south-eastern corner strengthened and erected a building, afterwards called the Karlsschanze (Carl's Entrenchment), which was topped by a mighty, five-storey tower and which was undertaken between 1681 and 1683. Only a few scraps of wall remain today to mark the place of the fortification.

The Thick Tower mentioned above was used by military engineers as a link between the north rampart – below the English Building – and Ludwig's mighty west wall. Roughly in the middle of the west flank, there was a semi-circular, thick-walled battery tower, the Rondell, which was an additional fortification. An arched

walk formed a connection between the lower storeys of the Rondell and the Thick Tower and led on through the north rampart to the cellar of the Friedrich Building. Two statues, similar to those on the Friedrich Building, represent the Palatine princes Ludwig V and Friedrich V.

In 1619, he had the rampart laid out as a pleasure garden and the Rondell party reduced to rubble. He presented the little triumphal arch to his wife, Elisabeth Stuart, in 1615 as a gift on her nineteenth birthday. One says that it was built in a night. A memorial tablet on the outer edge of the garden is dedicated to Goethe who was a guest in Heidelberg on seven occasions.

The huge earthworks and ramparts to the west were constructed by Ludwig V as a substitute for the earlier dungeon when this was rendered useless by building on top of it. From that time onwards the small fortified tower on the south-western corner served as a prison tower and received the cryptic epithet, «Seltenleer» – «rarely empty». In times of peace, the moat was used by its princely owner as a place in which to keep stags, but in times of danger it was filled with water.

The square Gate Tower, probably because of its form, was the only tower which withstood French attempts to blow it up. Measured from the bed of the moat below, it attains the respectable height of 52 metres. Its lower part served as a castle dungeon, Entry to the castle was secured by four doors, a formidable portcullis and a drawbridge. Its only decoration is that of two coarse-looking shield bearers and two smaller lions which at one time held the Palatine coats of arms which were probably of silver.

The inner rampart between the Gate Tower and the massive Powder Tower on the south-eastern corner was reinforced to seven metres thickness by Ludwig V. The mighty Gun Tower which was also called the Kraut-turm because of the gunpowder stocks in its cellar, seems almost exclusively constructed of brickwork. Despite this, its outer walls are 6.50 metres thick and it has a total diameter of 24 metres. It escaped the first attempts by the French to blow it up unscathed, only to yield to explosion four years later. On this occasion it split into two parts, the outer one falling into the moat and so providing us today with a view into the impressive interior of this colossal stronghold with its three storeys for artillery and the arches supported by a central pillar. To the east, the deep rift of the Friesen Valley offered a natural defence to would-be attackers before Friedrich V commissioned it to be changed into a splendid, landscaped terraced garden. In the wide angle of broken walling and the area of the Zwinger (dungeon) between the Powder Tower and the Bell Tower, another round tower was erected as reinforcement, the Apothecary's Tower. Around 1600, the castle owners built another storey above the old dungeon which had been in existence since the time of Friedrich II and fitted it out with a number of artillery positions in front of its outer wall. A covered sentry walk shut off the Friesen Valley on the south side of the moat. The topped casemate in front of the Apothecary's Tower, built after the Thirty Years War, signified a further step in the fortification of the eastern flank. The modification of the five terraces to accomodate the «Hortus Palatinus» or «Pfälzer Garten», nevertheless brought about a sensitive, weak point in the castle's defences. Thus, Friedrich V raised the bed of the valley some 20 metres.

Heidelberg's Old Town – Ecclesiastical Buildings

The centre of the Old Town is the giant Church of the Holy Ghost. The foundation stone of this church as it is today was laid by King Ruprecht of the Palatine around 1400. This, the largest Gothic, ecclesiastical building in the Palatinate of those days, as well as serving as a place of worship was also a place where the Palatine family were laid to rest and a place, too, for University celebrations. The roof as well as the tower was erected in baroque style by the Palatine prince, Johann Wilhelm, after damage caused by the War of Palatine Succession in 1693. Over the central portal towards the Hauptstraße, we find his coat of arms and that of his spouse, a woman of the Medici family, engraved in the stone. Inside the church we become aware of the varying intensity of light between that of the lighted choir and the dark nave. The reason for this is to be found in the galleries which were built later and which were to accomodate the considerable stocks of the Palatine Library, the famous «Bibliotheca Palatina». As the result of donations from noblemen and Palatine princes – Ottheinrich especially – as well as from Huldrich Fugger, all of them amounted to works weighing some 23,500 lbs (Translator's note: One German «Zentner» = 100 English pounds) and which at the same time contributed to the most well-stocked collection of books known to the world in those days.

In 1623, after Tilly had occupied the town, Duke Maximilian of Bavaria decreed that this, the most valuable collection of books known to western civilisation, be loaded as booty onto fifty carts together with the library stocks of the University and the private library of the Palatine princes and that it be donated to the Vatican as a gift. Only a small portion of these books were later restored or reclaimed.

Of the 55 Palatine graves desecrated in a fury of destruction by the soldiers of the Sun King in 1693, only those of King Ruprecht of the Pfalz († 1410) and his queen were left unharmed.

The oldest parish church in Heidelberg was the predecessor to the present Peterskirche (St Peter's Church) above Universitätsplatz (University Square). When the new building of the Church of the Holy Ghost was erected, around 1400, Ruprecht von der Pfalz released it from dependency on the smaller Church of St Peter and donated this to the University. The present, unpartitioned nave came into being before 1500. It accomodates the tombs of professors and important citizens from the 15th to the 19th centuries.

The Church of St Vitus in the Handschuhsheim district of the town contains interesting tombstones dating from the 14th century. On the Heiligenberg Hill district, one can still see the foundations of the old St Michael's Monastery, set up in the year 870 by monks from Lorsch and consecrated to All Hallows.

Public Buildings

The French invaders took their work of destruction so seriously — especially in 1693 — that within the old town of Heidelberg itself there is only very little left of its former building structure. The old Zeughaus, however, usually wrongly alluded to as the «Marstall» on the banks of the Neckar, remained intact. Today, it is used as a Mensa or students' refectory. Immediately after the destruction of the city, the building housing the Old University (Alte Universität) was erected on the spot bearing that name. It contains a large lecture theatre (Aula) in baroque style which is worth visiting.

The historic Studentenkarzer (students' jail) at the rear of the building was in use from 1712 until 1914.

The only remaining tower belonging to the town's defences has been included in the quadrangle to the rear of the New University which was erected in 1931. The fact that it served from time to time as a women's prison earned it the name «Hexenturm» (Witches' Tower).

The University Library (1905), situated at the upper end of Grabengasse, in addition to housing the German, handwritten manuscripts restored to it by the Vatican, also contains the famous Manesse manuscript which was re-acquired in 1888 from the Bibliothèque de Paris.

The Market Place, lying between the Church of the Holy Ghost and the baroque Town Hall (ca. 1700), served in the Middle Ages both as a centre of social life and also as a place of execution. Documents testify, for example, that here in the year 1525 «sevn to lose thir heeds & three fyr thir fingres to bee hackt off». Almost opposite, over the well in the Corn Market, a decorative, baroque Madonna stands, a masterpiece from the hand of Peter van den Brandens. The Corn Market Madonna is seen to especial effect when she is viewed against the silhouette of the castle in the background.

One of the most photographed objects in Heidelberg is the Karl Theodor Bridge, generally referred to as the Old Bridge. The towers themselves are still essentially those which were part of the town's medieval fortifications in the 13th century. The stone construction we see today was built by Karl Theodor in the years between 1786–88 in place of an original, wooden-roofed bridge standing only on stone pillars and which could be operated as a drawbridge at either end. The western tower contains three, dark dungeons, the eastern, one, and a spiral staircase. The statue to the town side depicts Karl Theodor, surrounded by the four river gods of his inherited lands: Rhine, Danube, Neckar and Moselle. Pallas Athene — godess of wisdom and protectress of castles and towns, keeps watch from a balcony on the northern side over piety, justice, agriculture and trade as well as astronomy, architecture, painting and the arts of sculpture and music. The statue at the head of the bridge to the north represents the patron saint of bridges, Nepomuk.

Burghers' houses

The soldiers of the «Sun King», Louis XIV of France, carried out their orders so scrupulously in their destruction of the Palatinate that the only citizen's house facade which dates back to a time before 1693 is that of the «Ritter» (Knight) in the Hauptstraße opposite the Church of the Holy Ghost. The Huguenot, Charles Belier, commissioned this splendid house to be erected in the year 1592 in the Renaissance style. Richly moulded decoration ornaments the insets of the projecting bay windows on both upper storeys.

After the razing of Heidelberg in 1693, its inhabitants returned only hesitantly to Heidelberg and began then to erect simple, new buildings upon the narrow foundations of their former Gohic-style houses. In this way, the medieval plan of the city was preserved, contrary to the plans of the Palatine princes. A few years later, how- ever, more distinguished houses came into existence such as that on the Karlsplatz, the Archduke's Palais (1717), since 1805 the city residence of the Archdukes of Baden, and the Palais Boisserée in which Goethe sojourned while visiting the town in the years 1814 and 1815. The Palais Moras, too, Hauptstraße 97, also came into being around 1712 as a distinguished manor house. The courtyard and garden radiate reflective peace even today. The interior, which is partly decorated with artistically moulded ceilings, is the repository today of the extensive collection of the Kurpfalz Museum.

Alleys and narrow houses characterize the town as well to the west of the Church of the Holy Ghost; Untere Straße, and the lanes adjacent to it, are examples. In one of the latter, Pfaffengasse, one finds the house in which Friedrich Ebert was born, the first German Reichspresident from 1919–1925.

Whoever keeps his eyes open while he strolls through the lanes of Heidelberg's Old Town will still be able to discover much that is charming in its detail, whether it be a baroque piece of sculpture placed in a niche on a house, a coat of arms or simply one of the many historical taverns. Despite the problems arising from its narrow streets and ageing private houses, Heidelberg has managed to remain a city, one indeed in which one can lose one's heart.

Les premiers temps de l'histoire

Le cours inférieure du Neckar fut déjà colonisé dans les temps les plus reculés. C'est en 1907 que les ouvriers d'une sablière trouvèrent dans les environs de Mauer, village situé à une quinzaine de kilomètres de Heidelberg, le plus vieux reste humain jamais découvert en Europe, la mâchoire inférieure du «homo heidelbergensis» âgé de 500.000 ans. A partir de 500 av. J.-C., les Celtes s'installèrent sur l'actuel emplacement de la ville. Pour arrêter l'avance des Germains, ils bâtirent une «Fliehburg», ou refuge fortifié, sur les deux sommets du Heiligenberg, ou montagne des Saints.

Lorsque les troupes de César atteignirent les rives du Neckar, les Celtes avaient déjà été délogés par les Germains et avaient émigré vers le sud. Peu après le début de l'ère chrétienne, les Romains construisirent un pont fixe sur le Neckar près de la vieille agglomération de Bergheim. Ils en assurèrent la défense par un castel édifié sur la rive droite du Neckar.

Heidelberg fait son entrée dans l'histoire

En l'an 1155, l'empereur Frédéric I, dit «Barberousse», conféra à son demi-frère Konrad von Hohenstaufen la dignité de comte palatin du Rhin. En 1214, l'empereur Frédéric II concéda le comté palatin à titre de tenure noble au duc Louis 1er de Bavière. Le comté demeura le fief de la famille Wittelsbach jusqu'au moment de la dissolution du Palatinat électoral en 1803. L'appellation «Heidelberch» est mentionnée pour la première fois en 1196 dans un document du monastère de Schönau. En 1225, Louis I (1214–28) obtint en fief un château fort situé à Heidelberg. Un château fort est de nouveau mentionné dans un document datant de 1294; en 1303, il est cependant question pour la première fois de deux places fortes. Le château d'en bas, édifié sur le Jettenbühl, fut à l'origine des fameuses ruines du château, alors que celui d'en haut se dressait sur le petit Gaisberg, l'emplacement de l'actuelle Molkenkur. Le château fort plus haut situé fut complètement détruit le 25 avril 1537, lorsque la foudre fit exploser les stocks de poudre considérables emmagasinés dans le corps de logis. En 1329, le traité de Pavie sanctionna la séparation des terres héréditaires du Palatinat électoral de la Bavière.

Le Palatinat électoral, puissance prédominante de l'Empire

Au cours de son long règne (1329–90), Ruprecht I parvint à renforcer la puissance et à rehausser le prestige du Palatinat électoral au point d'en faire l'une des principales forces de l'Empire. Lorsqu'en 1356, l'empereur Charles-Quint reconnut définitivement par la «Reichsgründungsgesetz», également appelé «Goldene Bulle», ou bulle d'or, le droit des sept princes électeurs d'élire les empereurs allemands, Ruprecht obtint également que la dignité électorale et la charge indivisible de grand écuyer (écuyer de cuisine et officier influent de la cour) fussent attribuées à lui-même et à ses descendants. Quelques années avant sa mort, il fonda l'université de Heidelberg (1386). Et lorsque son neveu Ruprecht III (1398–1410) accéda même au trône impérial (1401), l'étroit château ne suffit plus aux prétentions des princes, car l'on exigeait beaucoup d'une résidence aussi importante. C'est de cette époque que date le simple «Ruprechtsbau», ou bâtiment de Ruprecht, de style gothique.

Frédéric I, surnommé le Victorieux, que le peuple appelait également le «Fritz palatin», fut l'un des Electeurs les plus populaires. Son règne (1449–76) fut marqué d'une série de conflits armés. En plus de diffidations couronnées de succès, il remporta des victoires importantes à la bataille de Pfeddersheim (1460) et à Seckenheim (1462), ce qui lui valut la réputation d'être le plus grand chef militaire de son époque.

S'alliant aux Habsbourg, Louis V (1508–1544) participa victorieusement à la guerre provoquée par la succession de l'empereur Maximilien († 1519). La diffidation qui l'opposa aux Sickinger et les succès remportés dans la guerre des Paysans (1525) profitèrent considérablement à la dynastie des Electeurs palatins. C'est alors que Louis mit en chantier d'importantes activités de construction dans l'enceinte de son château résidentiel. Il commença par consolider les fortifications par la construction de nouveaux remparts et l'aménagement des tours et des murs d'enceinte. Il fit réparer ou reconstruire les bâtiments d'habitation et les communs entourant la cour du château. Sous le règne de Frédéric II (1544–1556) fut construit le «Gläserne Saalbau», ou salle de Glaces, qui marqua le début de la Renaissance au château des Electeurs. Avant de succéder à son oncle à Heidelberg, Othon-Henri, neveu de Frédéric, avait administré son petit duché de Pfalz-Neuenburg. Par la magnifique façade du «Ottheinrichsbau», palais qui porte son nom, il créa un modèle exemplaire de l'architecture Renaissance allemande.

Le comte palatin Jean-Casimir (1583–1592) superposa, il est vrai, le bâtiment du Tonneau au bastion nord, mais il fit bâtir, en revanche, la «Große Batterie», ou grande batterie, en guise de retranchement avancé du flanc nord. C'est sous le règne de son neveu Frédéric IV que le Palatinat devint la puissance prédominante du protestantisme en Allemagne. Dans la cour du château fut construit le «Friedrichsbau», ou palais de Frédéric, pendant réussi du palais d'Othon-Henri; ce nouveau bâtiment fut plus coûteux que le premier, quoique moins artistement orné. En faisant aménager le «Große Altan», ou grande terrasse, et en décidant, tout particulièrement, la construction de la façade extérieure du palais de Frédéric, il parvint à aérer élégamment l'imposante façade du château telle qu'on la voit de la vallée.

La décadence du Palatinat

Son fils Frédéric V (1610–1620) accéda dès sa prime jeunesse au trône électoral. Il ordonna la construction, sur le rempart nord, d'un simple bâtiment d'habitation, le «Englischer Bau», ou palais Anglais. Ses ambitions architecturales se concentrèrent cependant sur le jardin du château. Il chargea l'illustre architecte paysagiste Salomon de Caus de convertir les pentes nord et est entourant le château en un jardin en terrasses au goût du jour. Lorsqu'il accepta de se faire couronner roi de Bohème en 1619, la Guerre de Trente Ans s'enflamma définitivement. En conséquence de sa défaite à la bataille «am Weißen Berg», ou de la Montagne Blanche, Frédéric dut renoncer dès le mois de novembre de l'année suivante à sa royauté nouvellement acquise ainsi qu'à sa dignité héréditaire d'Electeur, il fut proscrit et se réfugia en Hollande. Il ne lui resta que le titre de «Winterkönig», ou roi des neiges, par lequel le désignent les historiens.

Le 26 août 1622, le général Tilly, commandant en chef des armées impériales, ordonna le canonnage du château et de la ville. Cette dernière fut prise d'assaut et investie le 16 septembre. La garnison du château capitula quelques jours plus tard. Pour la première fois dans l'histoire, la résidence des princes électeurs était tombée dans les mains de troupes ennemies.

Depuis le début des hostilités, les travaux de construction s'étaient limités à la réparation des bâtiments endommagés du château, de sorte que le palais Anglais demeura le dernier bâtiment à être construit à ce jour. Après que Frédéric V eut perdu ses terres et ses titres, ceux-ci échurent tout d'abord aux Wittelsbach de Bavière. La paix de Westphalie restitua au moins le patrimoine héréditaire au fils aîné de Frédéric, Charles-Louis (1649–1680). Le prince se mit patiemment et prudemment à reconstruire son pays ravagé et à éliminer du château ancestral les dégâts causés par la grande guerre. Son fils unique, Charles II (1680–1685), concentra son attention sur une consolidation des dispositifs de défense du château.

A sa mort et en raison de l'extinction de la lignée Pfalz-Simmern, le malheur dévasta de nouveau et plus que jamais le Palatinat. La soeur de Charles, Elisabeth-Charlotte, surnommée Liselotte du Palatinat, avait été mariée au duc d'Orléans, frère du roi Louis XIV de France. En son nom, mais sans son assentiment et en violation du droit relatif aux successions en vigueur, le roi-soleil exigea la cession à la France d'une grande partie du Palatinat. En octobre 1688, ses troupes investirent Heidelberg. Lorsque les armées des princes allemands alliés contre les Français approchèrent dangereusement, les soldats commandés par Mélac battirent en retraite en mars 1689, après avoir détruit toutes les fortifications et pressuré impitoyablement et le Palatinat et sa capitale, en exécution de l'ordre de leur conseil de guerre.

Entre-temps, Johann Wilhelm (1690–1716) avait accédé à la dignité de prince électeur et il stimula les habitants à remettre les fortifications rapidement en état. C'est ainsi que les troupes françaises purent être repoussées devant les murs de la ville en 1691 et 1692 respectivement. Le 22 mai 1693, Heidelberg tomba cependant une nouvelle fois aux mains des troupes étrangères et s'effondra dans un océan de flammes quelques heures à peine après la prise de la ville. Des bandes de soldats mirent la ville à sac et détruisirent aveuglément les monuments funéraires érigés avec art dans l'église du Saint-Esprit, ils profanèrent les tombes des princes électeurs, ils jetèrent leurs ossements sur la voie publique et emportèrent l'étain des cercueils en guise de trophée de guerre.

The extensive viewing terrace of the castle showing the Bell Tower (Glockenturm)
La grande terrasse du château et la tour de la Cloche
La gran terraza-mirador del castillo y la Glockenturm (→ Campanario)

Au château, ils se donnèrent toutes les peines du monde pour dynamiter les fortifications qui avaient échappé à la destruction en 1689, ils saccagèrent les palais, détruisirent ou firent main basse sur les trésors d'art et les provisions, et ils mirent le feu aux palais en utilisant des couronnes de résine.

Les Français partis, ce n'est que progressivement que les habitants de Heidelberg retournèrent dans leur ville et s'attelèrent à la construction de nouvelles maisons sur les soubassements des anciennes.

Peu après son avènement au trône, Charles-Philippe (1716–1742) se mit à restaurer les palais pour les rendre de nouveau habitables. En 1718, il transféra sa cour de Düsseldorf à Heidelberg. Ses projets d'une transformation à fond du château en y construisant une nouvelle aile accessoire sur le rempart occidental et une large route d'accès montant de la ville échouèrent tout d'abord faute d'argent et durent par la suite être définitivement abandonnés en raison des querelles avec la paroisse protestante à propos de l'utilisation de l'église du Saint-Esprit. En 1720, il déplaça sa résidence à Mannheim, où il se fit construire un vaste château.

Une deuxième tentative d'aménager le château de Heidelberg pour en faire de nouveau une résidence princière fut entreprise par l'Electeur Charles-Théodore (1742–1799). Le 24 juin 1764 cependant, lorsque la foudre frappa deux fois de suite la salle des Glaces et y provoqua un incendie qui s'étendit aux palais contigus, le prince y vit un avertissement du ciel et fit cesser les travaux. Le château de Heidelberg était devenu une fois pour toutes une ruine inhabitée.

A la mort de Charles-Théodore et l'extinction de la dernière branche de la première lignée électorale, le Palatinat fut de nouveau réuni à la Bavière en 1799, après 470 ans d'autonomie. La restructuration décidée en 1803 par les Etats de l'Empire, scella cependant définitivement le destin du Palatinat électoral: La rive gauche du Rhin dut être cédée à la France, une petite partie des terres situées sur la rive droite du Rhin revenant à Hessen-Darmstadt et le reste, Heidelberg compris, au grand-duché de Bade.

Les palais et communs du château des Electeurs

Le sobre palais de Ruprecht est le plus ancien des bâtiments conservés dans l'enceinte du château. Ce palais gothique pratiquement dénué de tout ornement fut construit sous l'Electeur Ruprecht III, le premier de son nom à régner sur l'empire allemand de 1400–1410. L'aigle impérial figurant à gauche de l'entrée rappelle la dignité royale du bâtisseur. L'oiseau tient dans ses serres les armoiries artistement travaillées des Wittelsbach, le Lion palatin et les Losanges bavarois.

Au-dessus de l'entrée se trouve un relief sculpté à même la clef de voûte, véritable chef d'oeuvre de l'art gothique: deux anges tenant une couronne de roses au centre de laquelle se trouve un compas.

Légèrement en retrait par rapport aux deux constructions voisines, le bâtiment de la Bibliothèque est le premier à avoir percé l'ancien anneau fortifié du château. Un ravissant encorbellement gothique orne la simple façade à hauteur du premier étage.

Le «Frauenzimmerbau» contigu, ou aile des Dames, dont on n'a conservé que le rez-de-chaussée, s'élevait jadis à la même hauteur. Le «Königssaal», ou salle du Roi, peut aujourd'hui contenir jusqu'à 700 personnes lors de réceptions et de représentations théâtrales.

Le magnifique palais Renaissance faisant face au «Torturm», ou tour du Portail, porte le nom de celui qui le fit construire: Frédéric (1592–1610). Les monumentales statues de chevaliers de la façade sud taillées dans le grès jaune représentent les aïeux du prince électeur. De gauche à droite nous voyons, dans la rangée supérieure, les ancêtres Charlemagne, Othon de Wittelsbach, Louis II et Rodolphe I, dans la deuxième rangée, des empereurs et des rois de la dynastie des Wittelsbach: Louis le Bavarois, Ruprecht du Palatinat, Othon de Hongrie et Christophe du Danemark. Les comtes palatins les plus importants de la vieille lignée palatine sont représentés par Ruprecht 1er, Frédéric le Victorieux et les bâtisseurs des palais Renaissance voisins, Frédéric II et Othon-Henri, qui sont placés dans les niches du premier étage. Entre les fenêtres de la chapelle du château se trouvent finalement les statues des princes électeurs de la branche Pfalz-Simmern: Frédéric III, Louis IV, Jean-Casimir et le bâtisseur lui-même, Frédéric IV. C'est aux étages supérieurs du palais de Frédéric que les princes électeurs avaient élu résidence. Restaurés avant 1900 sous la direction du professeur Karl Schäfer, ils nous donnent depuis une idée de nouveau très précise de la commodité robuste des appartements de la Renaissance.

C'est avec la salle des Glaces encastrée entre les célèbres façades richement ornées du palais de Frédéric et de l'aile Othon-Henri que les premiers éléments de la Renaissance apparaissent vers 1545 dans la résidence princière. Il tire son nom du «Festsaal», ou salle des fêtes, du premier étage, jadis garni jusque dans le moindre recoin de glaces vénitiennes. L'arc central situé entre les arcades porte les armes du bâtisseur, Frédéric II: le Lion palatin, les Losanges bavarois et, dans la troisième travée, le globe impérial que l'empereur Charles-Quint avait décerné à Frédéric en 1544 en symbole de sa dignité de grand Ecuyer de la cour. La façade du palais d'Othon-Henri qui réunit harmonieusement les éléments les plus divers est sans pareil au nord des Alpes. Des bandeaux artistement ornés et des demi-colonnes de formes différentes partagent la surface en panneaux réguliers, tous percés de deux contre-fenêtres séparées par une niche abritant une statue. Le portail richement décoré qui surplombe l'escalier extérieur ressemble à un arc de triomphe et s'orne d'un médaillon à l'image du prince Othon-Henri et, en outre, des armoiries de ce dernier et d'une inscription. Les fenêtres à croisées du rez-de-chaussée sont couronnées de frontons triangulaires contenant des pièces de monnaie romaines de la collection d'Othon-Henri, qui avait une passion pour l'art. A côté des atlantes du portail, nous trouvons dans la rangée inférieure, de gauche à droite: Josué, Samson, Hercule et David, héros de l'Ancien Testament. Les statues du premier étage symbolisent cinq des principales vertus: la Force (avec une colonne brisée), la Foi (avec une bible), l'Amour et la Maternité (avec des enfants), l'Espérance (avec une ancre) et la Justice (avec la balance et le glaive). Les sept personnages de la rangée supérieure représentent des divinités de la Rome antique que l'on a associées au soleil et à la lune, ainsi qu'aux cinq grandes planètes: Saturne, Mars, Vénus, Mercure et Diane et, par-dessus, Phébus et Jupiter qui se dressaient jadis devant deux frontons aujourd'hui disparus. Au rez-de-chaussée du palais d'Othon-Henri, ainsi qu'à l'intérieur du «Ludwigsbau» annexe, ou palais de Louis, et du «Apothekerturm», ou tour de l'Apothicaire, s'est installé le «Deutsches Apothekermuseum», ou musée allemand de la pharmacie, qui a trouvé ici un cadre convenable.

Les armoiries datant de 1524 et se trouvant sur la tour-escalier centrale évoquent le souvenir de Louis V, le grand bâtisseur du château. L'ancienne aile sud de son palais résidentiel est attenante aux communs, eux-mêmes contigus au porche de la Citerne et à la salle des gardes qui abrite de nos jours les guichets de réception du château.

A l'écart de la cour du château et à proximité de la grande terrasse se trouve l'étroit Faßbau, ou salle du Grand Tonneau, construit par Jean-Casimir (1583–1592) et surplombé de la petite terrasse. On y trouve aujourd'hui le Grand Tonneau de Charles-Théodore. Avec une contenance de 221 726 litres de vin, il est la plus grande cuve en bois utilisable du monde entier. Il a fallu 130 troncs de chêne pour la construction de cette cuve de 8,50 m de long et de 7 m de diamètre. Elle a pour unique ornement le grand blason sur lequel s'inscrivent les initiales de Charles-Théodore. A gauche du compas et du rabot que l'on utilisa au moment de la construction se trouve encore une partie de la conduite desservie par un dispositif de pompage et qui reliait le tonneau à la salle des fêtes de la salle du Roi. La petite statue est celle du nain Perkeo, gardien du tonneau et bouffon à la cour sous Charles-Philippe et Charles-Théodore. A en croire la légende, il passa de vie à trépas après s'être laissé persuader d'avaler un verre d'eau à la place de son vin habituel. De nos jours encore, il est le patron symbolique du carnaval de Heidelberg.

La légende nous rapporte que la trace d'une botte sur l'une des dalles de grès de la grande terrasse y fut empreinte par un chevalier éconduit qui aurait sauté en armure de la fenêtre de sa dulcinée située à l'étage supérieur du palais de Frédéric.

Les fortifications du château de Heidelberg

Une attaque lancée du nord ou de l'ouest semblait la moins dangereuse, la pente escarpée y constituant une protection naturelle. On n'en trouve pas moins à l'angle nord-ouest le «Dicker Turm», ou Grosse Tour, la plus puissante des tours du château en raison de son diamètre de 30 m. L'explosion déclenchée par le minage de la tour en emporta une partie, n'épargnant que la moitié adossée à la montagne. A voir celle-ci, nous avons une idée de l'efficacité passée de ce bastion imposant dont les murs sont d'une épaisseur de 7 m. Au XVIIe siècle, Frédéric V en fit démolir la partie supérieure à colombage et la remplaça par une salle des fêtes et de théâtre de forme polygonale dont les parois, faute de place, étaient de faible épaisseur et entrecoupées de hautes fenêtres. Il obtint ainsi une salle de bal de plus de 500 m² directement contiguë à son palais, le bâtiment Anglais.

Prévu comme un élément des fortifications, le Glockenturm, ou tour de la Cloche, construit dans l'angle nord-est ne comprenait à l'origine qu'un seul étage. Par la suite, les princes électeurs firent ajouter plusieurs étages à des fins résidentielles.

La «grande batterie» avait été construite en avant de la grande terrasse pour accueillir les pièces d'artillerie. Le prince électeur Charles fit fortifier l'angle sud-est par la contruction, dans les années 1681–83, de la «Karls-schanze», ou retranchement de Charles, et du massif «Batterieturm», ou tour de la Batterie, haut de cinq étages et dont il ne reste plus que quelques pans de mur insignifiants.

La Grosse Tour dont il a déjà été question assurait la jonction entre le rempart nord – au-dessous de l'aile Anglaise – et le puissant rempart ouest construit par Charles V. Vers le milieu du rempart ouest se dressait une tour de batterie additionnelle semi-circulaire aux murs épais, surnommée la Rondelle. Un passage voûté reliait les étages inférieurs de la Rondelle et de la Grosse Tour et conduisait, en outre, au sous-sol de l'aile Frédéric à travers le rempart nord. Deux statues semblables à celles de l'aile Frédéric représentent les princes électeurs Louis V et Frédéric V.

En 1619, Frédéric fit transformer le terre-plein en un jardin d'agrément et il fit combler la Rondelle en partie. En 1615, à l'occasion de son dix-neuvième anniversaire, il offrit à son épouse Elisabeth Stuart la porte Elisabeth, petit arc de triomphe que Frédéric aurait fait élever en une nuit, nous rapporte la légende. Une plaque commémorative fixée à l'ouest du «Stückgarten», ou jardin des Canons, est dédiée à Johann Wolfgang Goethe qui séjourna à Heidelberg à sept reprises.

Louis V avait fait élever un imposant terre-plein et creuser les profonds fossés pour prendre le relai de l'ancien donjon devenu inefficace en conséquence de transformations architecturales. La petite tour de défense de l'angle sud-ouest fut depuis utilisée comme prison et baptisée «Seltenleer», ce qui signifie «rarement vide». Les fossés abritaient des cerfs en temps de paix et étaient remplis d'eau en périodes troublées.

Le «Torturm», ou tour du Portail, a sans doute été le seul à résister aux tentatives de minage des Français en raison de sa forme quadratique. Du fond des fossés, elle atteint la hauteur respectable de 52 mètres. Au sous-sol se trouvaient les oubliettes du château. La défense de l'entrée était assurée par quatre portes, une herse imposante et un pont-levis. Cette tour a pour unique décoration deux écuyers en pierre à l'aspect rude et petits lions qui tenaient l'écusson – probablement en argent – des princes électeurs.

Louis V fit renforcer le rempart intérieur dont l'épaisseur atteignit alors 7 m entre la tour du Portail et le monumental «Pulverturm», ou tour de la Poudrière, bâti dans l'angle sud-est. La puissante tour d'artillerie – également surnommée «Krautturm» à cause de la poudrière installée au rez-de-chaussée – semble se constituer presque uniquement de maçonnerie tant les murs en sont épais, ces derniers n'ayant pas moins de 6,50 m d'épaisseur contre 24 m de diamètre seulement. Elle résista sans dommage aux premières tentatives de minage des Français en 1689, mais y succomba quatre ans plus tard. En 1693, la charge explosive ayant été plus forte, elle se fendit en deux, un pan du mur s'affaissant dans le fossé. C'est ainsi qu'émergea au grand jour la vue imposante de l'intérieur du colosse à trois étages dont les voûtes prennent appui sur le pilier central.

A l'est, le château était protégé par les pentes abruptes de la vallée de la Frise jusqu'à ce que Frédéric V les fît transformer en un magnifique jardin en terrasses. Les remparts et les fossés tracés en angle obtus entre la tour de la Poudrière et la tour de la Cloche sont, en outre, fortifiés par la tour de l'Apothicaire circulaire. Vers 1600, les seigneurs du château entamèrent la construction d'un nouveau donjon, équipé de plusieurs positions d'artillerie en avant du mur extérieur, pour remplacer le vieux donjon que Frédéric II avait fait surélever d'un étage. Un chemin de ronde couvert bouclait la vallée de la Frise du côté sud du fossé. La casemate construite devant la tour de l'Apothicaire après la guerre de Trente Ans constituait une nouvelle fortification du long tronçon du flanc oriental.

Le remblayage des cinq terrasses destinées à la création du «Hortus Palatinus» – jardin Palatin – entraîna, en revanche, un affaiblissement sensible des dispositifs de défense du château. Pour réaliser ses projets, Frédéric fit combler la vallée de la Frise jusqu'à 20 m de hauteur.

La vieille ville de Heidelberg
Edifices religieux

Au centre de la ville se dresse l'imposante «Heiliggeistkirche», ou église du Saint-Esprit. C'est vers 1400 que le roi Ruprecht du Palatinat posa la première pierre de l'actuelle église à trois nefs. Ce temple qui est la plus grande des églises gothiques de l'ancien Palatinat électoral tenait lieu de sépulture à la famille électorale, ainsi que de salle des cérémonies de l'université. Après les destructions occasionnées par la guerre de Succession du Palatinat (1693), le prince électeur Jean-Guillaume fit construire l'actuel toit de même que le clocher en style baroque. Du côté de la Hauptstraße, ou rue principale, on peut voir, gravées au-dessus du portail central, ses armoiries et celles de son épouse, une princesse Medici.

A l'intérieur de l'église, on s'aperçoit des différences de luminosité entre le choeur clair et la grande nef sombre. Ce phénomène est dû aux tribunes construites après coup et destinées à accueillir l'importante bibliothèque palatine, la fameuse «Bibliotheca Palatina». Alors la plus grande collection de livres du monde, cette bibliothèque fut créée grâce aux dons de plusieurs nobles et princes électeurs, notamment Othon-Henri, ainsi qu'à la donation de Huldrich Fugger, qui lui légua des oeuvres d'un poids total de 235 quintaux.

Après la prise de la ville par Tilly en 1623, le duc Maximilien de Bavière fit don au pape de la plus précieuse collection de livres du monde occidental en même temps que de la bibliothèque de l'université et des collections privées des princes électeurs, et il ordonna que ce butin de guerre fût transporté au Vatican sur cinquante chariots. Par la suite, seule une petite partie en fut restituée ou rachetée.

Des 55 tombeaux des princes électeurs livrés au vandalisme des soldats du roi-soleil en 1693, il ne reste que celui du roi Ruprecht du Palatinat († 1410) et de son épouse.

La plus vieille église paroissiale de Heidelberg se situait sur l'emplacement de l'actuelle église Saint-Pierre, en haut de la place de l'Université. C'est seulement une fois la reconstruction de l'église du Saint-Esprit terminée – vers 1400 – que Ruprecht du Palatinat la délia de sa dépendance de la petite église Saint-Pierre qu'il subordonna à l'université. L'actuelle église à une seule nef date d'avant 1500. Elle abrite les tombeaux de professeurs et citoyens célèbres du XVe au XIXe siècle.

L'église Saint-Vitus, située dans le quartier de Handschuhsheim, contient des monuments funéraires qui datent d'après le XIVe siècle et valent la peine d'êtres vus.

Sur le Heiligenberg, ou montagne des Saints, situé en haut de Handschuhsheim, se trouvent encore les fondations du vieux monastère Saint-Michel, fondé en 870 par des moines de Lorsch et consacré à «tous les saints».

Edifices publics

Les troupes françaises prirent leur oeuvre de destruction à ce point au sérieux, surtout en 1693, qu'il ne reste guère dans l'enceinte du vieux Heidelberg de constructions édifiées avant cette date. Ainsi fut épargné le vieux «Zeughaus», ou arsenal, situé au bord du Neckar et aujourd'hui dénommé à tort «Marstall», ou écurie. Il abrite à présent la «Mensa», ou cantine de l'université.

Immédiatement après la destruction de la ville, le bâtiment de «l'ancienne université» fut consltruit sur l'emplacement du même nom. Il renferme une «aula», ou salle des actes et des fêtes, aux ornements baroques qui vaut la peine d'être visitée. L'historique «Studentenkarzer», ou cachot des étudiants, situé derrière le bâtiment de «l'ancienne université», a été utilisé entre 1712 et 1914.

Dans la cour de la «nouvelle université» construite en 1931, on a inséré dans le mur la seule tour des fortifications de la ville qui ait survécu. Des femmes y ayant parfois été emprisonnées, elle fut surnommée «Hexenturm», ce qui signifie «tour des Sorcières». Edifiée au bout de la «Grabengasse», ou rue du Fossé, la bibliothèque de l'université (1905) abrite de nouveau, en plus des manuscrits allemands restitués par le Vatican, le fameux manuscrit «Manesse», qui put être racheté en 1888 de la Bibliothèque de Paris.

La place du Marché entre l'église du Saint-Esprit et la partie centrale baroque de l'hôtel de ville était au moyen âge à la fois le centre de la vie mondaine et un lieu de supplice. Des documents prouvent qu'en 1525 «sept personnes furent décapitées et trois autres eurent la main coupée».

En traversant la rue en biais, nous arrivons devant la fontaine du Kornmarkt, ou Marché aux Grains, ornée d'une statue baroque de la Vierge, chef d'oeuvre de Peter van den Branden. Le charme de la Madonne du Marché aux Grains est particulièrement rehaussé par la silhouette du château en arrière-plan.

Le pont Charles-Théodore, le plus souvent surnommé «Alte Brücke», ou Vieux-Pont, est l'un des monuments les plus photographiés de Heidelberg. Les deux tours sont en fait des vestiges des fortifications de la ville médiévale du XIIIe siècle. Charles-Théodore fit construire le pont en pierre pour remplacer un pont en bois couvert qui avait simplement reposé sur des piliers de pierre et dont les extrémités étaient pourvues de ponts-levis.

Côté ville, nous voyons la statue de Charles-Théodore entourée des figures allégoriques des quatre rivières traversant ses terres: le Rhin, le Danube, le Neckar et la Moselle. Côté nord c'est Pallas Athénée, déesse de la sagesse et déesse tutélaire des châteaux et des villes, qui veille sur la Piété, la Justice, l'Agriculture et le Commerce, de même que sur l'Astronomie, l'Architecture, la Peinture, la Sculpture et la Musique. La statue qui se trouve à l'extrémité nord du pont représente saint Népomucène, le saint patron des ponts.

Les maisons bourgeoises

Les soldats du roi-soleil, Louis XIV de France, exécutèrent si minutieusement l'ordre de raser le Palatinat que la façade d'une seule maison bourgeoise datant d'avant 1693 put être préservée à Heidelberg; il s'agit du «Ritter», ou maison du Chevalier, situé en face de l'église du Saint-Esprit. En 1592, le huguenot Charles Belier avait fait construire ce magnifique bâtiment dans le style de la Renaissance. De riches décorations ornent surtout les parties en saillie des deux premiers étages.

Après la destruction totale de la ville en 1693, les habitants hésitèrent à revenir à Heidelberg et les nouvelles maisons qu'ils édifièrent étaient de construction simple et le plus souvent bâties sur les fondations de leurs anciennes maisons gothiques. Cela permit de conserver la coupe horizontale du moyen âge à l'encontre des plans du prince électeur. Quelques années plus tard, on se mit cependant à construire également des édifices plus généreusement conçus, tels le «Großherzogliches Palais» (1717), ou palais Grand-Ducal, qui se trouve sur la place du Marché aux Grains et a servi de résidence aux grands-ducs de Bade à partir de 1805, lors de leurs séjours à Heidelberg, ou encore le palais Boisserée où Goethe séjourna en 1814 et 1815. De même, le palais Morass, situé au 97 de la Grand'Rue et édifié en 1712, était destiné à être une élégante maison seigneuriale. La cour et le jardin respirent toujours une paix contemplative. Les salles intérieures ornées en partie de plafonds en stuc artistement travaillés abritent l'importante collection du «Kurpfälzisches Museum», ou musée du Palatinat électoral.

Des ruelles et des maisons étroites sont également caractéristiques des quartiers situés à l'ouest de l'église du Saint-Esprit, notamment dans la «Untere Straße», ou rue du Bas, et les ruelles adjacentes. C'est dans l'une d'elles, la «Pfaffengasse», ou rue des Prêtres, que se trouve la maison natale de Friedrich Ebert, premier président de la République de Weimar de 1919 à 1925.

En flânant les yeux grands ouverts à travers les rues de la vieille ville de Heidelberg, on peut encore découvrir maint détail charmant, qu'il s'agisse d'une sculpture baroque dans la niche d'une maison, d'un écusson ou de l'un des nombreux établissements historiques. En dépit des problèmes auxquels il se voit confronté en raison de ses immeubles d'habitation démodés et ses rues étroites, Heidelberg est demeuré une ville dont on peut s'éprendre.

Edad Antigua

Ya en la más remota antigüedad se hallaron pobladas las zonas bajas del Néckar. En 1907, unos trabajadores de una mina de arena encontraron en Mauer – pueblo situado a unos 15 kilometros de Heidelberg – el maxilar inferior del «homo heidelbergensis» que, con sus 550.000 años de existencia, constituye el resto humano más antiguo de Europa. Quinientos años aproximadamente antes de nuestra era cristiana, tribus celtas habitaron la zona en que se encuentra hoy en día la ciudad. Para defenderse contra los avances germanos edificaron un refugio fortificado sobre las dos colinas con las que culmina el Monte Sacro (→ Heiligenberg). Cuando las legiones de César llegaron a las zonas del bajo Néckar, los celtas ya habían sido expulsados de sus territorios por los germanos y emigrado hacia el Sur. Pocos años despues del comienzo de la nueva era, y en las inmediaciones de la vieja colonia Bergheim, los romanos construyeron sobre el Néckar un puente consistente. Este estaba protegido por un castillo edificado en la margen derecha del río Néckar.

Aparición de Heidelberg en el escenario histórico

En 1155, el emperador Federico I – «Barbarroja» – concedió a su hermanastro Conrado de Hohenstaufen la dignidad de conde palatino del Rín (→ ringrave). En 1214, el emperador Federico II otorgó en feudo el condado palatino al duque de Baviera Luís I, de la dinastía de los Wittelsbacher. Quedó en posesión de la familia hasta la disolución del Electorado Palatino en el año 1803. El nombre «Heidelberch» aparece por primera vez en 1196 en un documento del convento de Schönau. En el año 1225, Luís I (1214–1228) obtuvo en feudo un castillo en Heidelberg. Documentos auténticos del año 1294 ya mencionan la existencia de un castillo. En el año 1303, sin embargo, ya son dos los castillos mencionados. El de abajo, situado en el Jettenbühl, constituyó los orígines de las actuales ruinas. El castillo superior, situado en el Kleiner Gaisberg, se hallaba en el lugar que ocupa actualmente la «Molkenkur» (restaurante de fama mundial). La fortificación superior quedó totalmente destruída el 25 de abril de 1537 debido a la explosion, provocada por un rayo, de las enormes reservas de pólvora almacenadas en el edificio central. En el año 1329, con el «Hausvertrag von Pavía» (→ Tratado de Pavía), los patrimonios palatinos dejaron de pertenecer a Baviera.

El Electorado Palatino, la primera autoridad del reino

Durante su largo reinado (1329–1390), Ruperto I logró convertir el Palatinado, por su poder y prestigio, en una de las primeras fuerzas del imperio. Cuando en las Dietas del Imperio de Nuremberg y Metz, 1356, el emperador Carlos IV, por la Ley fundamental del Reino – llamada «Bula de Oro» – confirmaba definitivamente a los siete príncipes electores como encargados de la elección de los reyes alemanes (por ello llamados Electores), Ruperto obtuvo para sí y para sus sucesores, en calidad de propiedad indivisible, la dignidad de Elector y el título de Mayordomo Mayor del Imperio (Mayordomo de cocina y funcionario de mayor influencia en la corte). Pocos años antes de su muerte fundó la Universidad de Heidelberg (1386). Cuando en 1401 fué coronado rey su nieto Ruperto III (1398–1410), el pequeño castillo no bastaba para cubrir las elevadas exigencias propias de una residencia tan importante. De ésta época data la sencilla construcción gótica Ruprechtbau (→ Construcción Ruperta).

Uno de los príncipes electores de mayor popularidad fué Federico I el Victòrioso – en lenguaje popular llamado «Pfälzer Fritz» (→ «Fede el Palatino»). Su reinado (de 1449 a 1476) estuvo caracterizado por un sinfín de enfrentamientos y luchas. Sus éxitos bélicos y las importantes victorias conseguidas en Pfeddersheim (1460) y Seckenheim (1462) le proporcionaron la fama de ser el mejor héroe militar de su tiempo.

A la muerte del emperador Maximiliano († 1519), y con motivo de la sucesión, estalló una guerra. Luís V (1508-1544) lucho en favor de la casa de los Austrias y concluyó la guerra victoriosamente. Las luchas contra la casa de los Sickingen y los éxitos obtenidos en la Guerra de los Labradores (1525) aumentaron todavía más el prestigio de la casa de los Electores. Luís V comenzó entonces a construir activamente en su castillo residencial. Reforzó, en primer lugar, las fortificaciones con nuevas instalaciones, emplió la muralla y construyó más torreones. Las viviendas y edificios destinados a la administración situados en torno al patio del castillo fueron restaurados o edificados de nuevo.

Durante el reinado de Federico II (1544–1556) fué construído el edificio del Salón de los Espejos (→ Gläserner Saalbau). Con ello introdujo el estilo renacentista en el castillo electoral.

Ottheinrich (1556–1559), sobrino de Federico, había gobernado el pequeño ducado de Pfalz-Neuburg hasta que tomó la posesión de su cargo en Heidelberg. Con la maravillosa fachada de la construcción que lleva su nombre (→ Ottheinrichsbau) creó un modelo ejemplar de la arquitectura renacentista germana. El conde palatino Juan Casimiro (1583–1592) construyó sobre la ronda norte el edificio de la bodega (→ Faß-bau); en su lugar, sin embargo, instaló la Gran Batería (→ Große Batterie) como posición avanzada de defensa del flanco norte. Durante el reinado de su sobrino Federico IV, el Palatinado se convirtió en el propulsor del Protestantismo en Alemania. Combinando perfectamente con la construcción Ottheinrich, se construyó en el patio del castillo el edificio Friedrichsbau. Construcción también costosa, si bién no tan artística como la anterior. Sin embargo, y visto desde el valle, consiguió mediante la gran terraza y especialmente mediante la fachada exterior de la construcción Friedrichsbau una perfecta distribución de la imponente parte frontal del castillo.

Decadencia del Palatinado

Federico V (1610–1620), su hijo, alcanzó la dignidad electoral siendo todavía muy joven. En la muralla norte, mandó construir una sencilla vivienda: la Construcción Inglesa (→ Englischer Bau). El principal objetivo, sin embargo, de sus actividades arquitectónicas fueron los jardines del palacio. A Salomón de Caus, famoso constructor de jardines, le dió el encargo de transformar en terrazas las laderas norte y este del castillo. Cuando en 1619 se hizo elegir rey de Bohemia, estalló definitivamente la Guerra de los Treinta Años. En noviembre del año siguiente, Federico fué vencido en la decisiva batalla de Weisser Berg (→ Monte Blanco, en Praga) y, con ello, perdió la dignidad real recientemente adquirida y su heredada dignidad electoral. Se le desterró y huyo a Holanda. No le quedó otro título que el de «Winterkönig» (→ Rey de invierno) con el que pasó a la historia.

El 26 de agosto de 1622 el general Tilly, jefe supremo de las tropas imperiales, abrió el fuego contra el castillo y la ciudad. El 16 de septiembre tomó por asalto la ciudad. Pocos días despues se entregó la guarnición que defendía el castillo. La residencia electoral cayó, por primera vez, en poder de tropas enemigas.

Desde el comienzo de la Guerra de los Treinta Años, los trabajos de construcción en el castillo se habían limitado a restaurar las construcciones deterioradas. El «Englischer Bau» (→ Construcción Inglesa) siguió siendo – hasta hoy – la última vivienda construida. Al perder Federico V los territorios y la dignidad electoral, pasaron ambos, en un principio, a manos de la dinastía bávara de los Wittelsbacher. Al firmarse la Paz de Westfalia, Karl Ludwig (1649–1680), hijo de Federico, recobró de nuevo los patrimonios perdidos. Con paciencia y circunspección comenzó a reconstruir el devastado territorio y a restaurar los daños existentes en la residencia palaciega de sus antepadados. Carlos II (1680–1685), hijo único suyo, concentró toda su atención en reforzar las fortificaciones defensivas del castillo.

A su muerte, y al extinguirse el linaje de los Pfalz-Simmern, cayó sobre el Palatinado de nuevo la desgracia y, ahora, con mayor fuerza que nunca. Isabel Carlota, hermana de Carlos, llamada Liselotte von der Pfalz, había contraído matrimonio con el duque de Orleans, hermano del rey francés Luís XIV. En su nombre, pero sin su consentimiento y contra el derecho de heredad vigente, exigió el «Rey Sol» la entrega de una gran parte del Palatinado. En 1688, sus tropas invadieron Heidelberg. Al acercarse amenazantes los ejércitos de los príncipes palatinos, aliados contra los franceses, las tropas francesas, dirigidas por Mélac, se retiraron en marzo de 1689 después de – de acuerdo con la órden del consejo de guerra – haber destruído todas las fortificaciones y haber saqueado totalmente todo el Palatinado, incluso su capital. Entretanto Johan Wilhelm (1690–1716) se había convertido en príncipe elector e incitó a la población a restaurar inmediatamente las fortificaciones destruídas. De esta forma, y debido a los muros de la ciudad, las tropas francesas pudieron ser rechazadas una y otra vez en 1691 y 1692. El 22 de mayo de 1693, sin embargo, Heidelberg cayó de nuevo en manos de tropas extranjeras. Pocas horas despues de la toma de la ciudad, Heidelberg parecía un océano de llamas. La soldadesca saqueó la ciudad, destruyó absurdamente los monumentos fúnebres de la iglesia del Espíritu Santo (→ Heiliggeistkirche), desenterraron los restos mortales de los príncipes electores, los esparcieron

An aerial view of the Castle.
Vue aérienne du château.
Vista aérea del castillo.

25

The Elizabeth Gate in the Gun Park on the former western rampart.
La porte Elisabeth et le jardin des Canons sur l'ancien rempart ouest.
La Elisabethentor en el jardín Stückgarten (→ Jardín de artillería), en el antiguo bastión oeste.

Views of the castle ruins from the Stückgarten.
Vue depuis le «Stückgarten» sur les ruines du château.
Vistas desde el Stückgarten sobre las ruinas del castillo.

The castle yard with the Friedrich Building, the Glass Hall Building, bell tower and well room.
La cour du château avec l'aile Frédéric, la salle des glaces, le clocher et le pavillon du puits.
Patio del castillo con el edificio Friedrichsbau, el gran salón de cristal, el campanario y la sala de la fuente.

27

Overlooking the great castle terrace.
Vue sur la grande terrasse du château.
Vista sobre la galería del castillo.

Gallery on the 2nd floor of the Friedrich building.
Galerie du 2è étage de l'aile Frédéric.
Pasillo en el 2° piso superior del edificio Friedrichsbau.

Passage on the courtyard side on the 1st floor of the Friedrich Building.
Couloir côté cour du 1er étage de l'aile Frédéric.
Pasillo junto al lado del patio del 1er piso superior en el edificio Friedrichsbau.

Prince's apartment in the Friedrich Building with Nuremberg tiled stove.
Appartement princier dans l'aile Frédéric avec poêle en faïence de Nuremberg.
Habitación de los príncipes en el edificio Friedrichsbau con estufa de azulejos de Nürnberg.

The statue of the vat's guardian, Perkeo.
Une statue de Perkeo, gardien du tonneau.
Una estatua del vigilante del tonel: Perkeo.

Das war der Zwerg Perkeo
Im Heidelberger Schloß,
An Wuchse klein und winzig,
An Durste riesengroß.

VICTOR VON SCHEFFEL

The Great Vat (cap. 221,726 litres). ▷
Le Grand Tonneau (221 726 l.).
El gran tonel (221 726 litros).

The courtyard facade of the Friedrich Building showing statues of princes of the Palatine.
Façade sud de l'aile Frédéric avec les statues des princes électeurs.
Portada de la construcción Friedrichsbau con estatuas de los príncipes electores.

The decorative Renaissance palace of the Kurfürst Ottheinrich (1556–1559). ▷
Le palais Renaissance artistement orné de l'Electeur Othon-Henri.
El artístico palacio renacentista del príncipe elector Ottheinrich (1556–1559).

View from the Molkenkur towards the Palatine castle and Neckar.
Le château des Electeurs et le Neckar vus de la Molkenkur.
Vista del castillo electoral y del río Néckar desde la Molkenkur.

The ruins of the Powder Tower at the south-eastern corner of the castle grounds. ▷
La tour de la Poudrière à l'angle sud-est des remparts.
Ruinas de la torre del polvorín (→ Pulverturm) en el ángulo sudeste de la fortaleza.

«Father Rhine» and the play of water in front of the Large Grotto.
«Vater Rhein», figure allégorique du Rhin entourée de jets d'eau devant la Grande Grotte.
«Vater Rhein» con la fuente de surtidores delante de la Gran Gruta.

◁ *Autumn idyll in the castle grounds.*
L'idylle de l'automne dans le jardin du château.
Idilio otoñal en los jardines del castillo.

View from the eastern side of the garden promenade in the Hortus Palatinus.
Le château vu de la promenade du Hortus Palatinus.
Aspecto de la avenida este del jardín Hortus Palatinus.

In the castle garden.
Dans les jardins du château.
En el jardín del castillo.

The Goethe monument.
Monument à la mémoire de Goethe.
Monumento a Goethe.

The Old Town of Heidelberg.
La vieille ville de Heidelberg.
Altstadt (Casco viejo de Heidelberg).

View onto the sturdy bulk of the Church of the Holy Ghost and the Old Bridge.
Vue sur l'imposante église du Saint-Esprit et le Vieux-Pont.
Vista de la majestuosa iglesia Heiliggeistkirche y del Puente Viejo.

por las calles y se llevaron consigo como botín de guerra el estaño de los ataúdes. Con dificultades, consiguieron volar las fortificaciones del castillo que se habían salvado de la destrucción de 1689, saquearon los palacios, robaron o deshicieron los tesoros artísticos y provisiones y, con ayuda de aros embreados, prendieron fuego a las residencias palaciegas.

Lentamente, y despues de la retirada de los franceses, regresaron los heidelberguenses a su destruida ciudad y comenzaron a edificar de nuevo sobre los fundamentos de las casas anteriores.

Karl Philipp (1716–1742), poco despues de la toma de posesión de su cargo, intentó de nuevo hacer habitables los palacios. En el año 1718 trasladó su residencia de Dusseldorf a Heidelberg. Sus proyectos de reconstruir totalmente el castillo, mediante un nuevo y prolongado tramo en el bastión oeste y la construcción de una ancha calle de acceso desde la ciudad, fracasaron en un principio por falta de dinero y luego, definitivamente, dadas las desavenencias con la comunidad evangélica a causa de la utilización de la iglesia del Espíritu Santo (→ Heiliggeistkirche). En 1720 trasladó su residencia a Mannheim donde se construyó un suntuoso palacio. El último intento de transformar el castillo nuevamente en una digna residencia, corrió a cargo del príncipe elector Karl Theodor (1742–1799). Sin embargo, y dado que durante los trabajos de renovación cayeron en la construcción del Salón de los Espejos (→ Gläserner Saalbau) dos rayos seguidos – el 24 de junio de 1764 – e incendiaron tanto éste como los palacios adyacentes, el soberano vió en ello un aviso del cielo y mandó interrumpir los trabajos. El castillo de Heidelberg se convirtió así, definitivamente, en ruína inanimada.

A la muerte de Karl-Theodor, y con la desaparición del último de los descendientes de la antigua dinastía de los Electores, el Palatinado quedó anexionado a Baviera en 1799 despues de 470 años de independencia. En 1803, el Tribunal Supremo de la Diputación del Imperio selló definitivamente el destino del Palatinado: los territorios de la margen izquierda del Rín debían pasar a poder de los franceses; una parte pequeña de los territorios situados en la margen derecha del Rín, pasaban al Gran Ducado Hesse-Darmstad y la mayor parte, incluido Heidelberg, a Baden.

Los palacios y dependencias adminstativas del castillo de los Electores

La obra arquitectónica más antigua en el recinto del castillo es la sencilla Construcción Ruperta (→ Ruprechtsbau), situada enfrente de las taquillas del castillo. El palacio gótico, casi sin ornamentación alguna, fué construído en tiempos del príncipe Elector Ruperto III – soberano alemán (desde 1400 hasta 1410) con el nombre de Ruperto I el Palatino. El águila imperial, a la izquierda de la entrada, alude a la dignidad real de su dueño. En sus garras, y maravillosamente trabajados, el ave sostiene los blasones familiares de los Wittelsbacher: el león palatino y los rombos bávaros.

Sobre la entrada, y haciendo las veces de dovela, encontramos una magistral escultura gótica: una pareja de angeles con una guirnalda de rosas y, encerrado en ella, un círculo.

El edificio de la biblioteca (→ Bibliotheksbau), en relación a las dos construcciones contiguas un tanto pospuesto, fué la obra arquitectónica más antigua que interceptaba el antiguo cinturón amurallado de la fortaleza. Un elegante mirador gótico, situado a la altura del primer piso, adorna la sencilla fachada.

También a la misma altura se hallaban en otro tiempo, a continuación, las dependencias de las mujeres de servicio (→ Frauenzimmerbau). Del edificio se conserva hoy, únicamente, la planta baja. El «Salón del rey» (→ Königssaal), dedicado a festivales y representaciones teatrales, tiene una capacidad para setecientas personas. El magnífico palacio renacentista, enfrente de la Torturm (→ torre con puerta de acceso), lleva el nombre de su constructor: Federico IV (1592–1610). Las monumentales estatuas de los caballeros nobles situadas en la fachada interior, en arenisca amarilla, representan a los antepasados de los Electores. La hilera superior, de izquierda a derecha, muestra a Carlomagno, Otto de Wittelsbach, Luís II y Rodolfo I (ascendientes suyos). La otra hilera está compuesta por emperadores y reyes de la dinastía de los Wittelsbacher: Luís el Bávaro, Ruperto el Palatino, Otto de Ungría y Cristobal de Dinamarca. Los condes palatinos más importantes del linaje de los Electores (Ruperto I, Federico el Victorioso y los constructores de los palacios renacentistas contiguos: Federico II y Ottheinrich) los hallamos en las hornacinas de las ventanas del primer piso. Finalmente, y entre las ventanas de la capilla del castillo, se hallan los príncipes Electores de la línea Pfalz-Simmern: Federico III, Luís VI, Johan Kasimir y el constructor del edificio, Federico IV.

Los pisos altos de la construcción Friedrichsbau eran la residencia palaciega de la familia de los príncipes electores. Bajo la dirección del profesor Karl Schäfer fueron restaurados antes del año 1900 y, desde entonces, ofrecen nuevamente una imagen impresionante del genuíno confort doméstico en la época del renacimiento. La construcción del Salón de los Espejos (→ Gläserner Saalbau), situada entre las dos majestuosas fachadas de las construcciones Friedrichsbau y Ottheinrichbau – más modernas y ornamentadas con figuras – introdujo en la residencia lectoral los primeros elementos renacentistas. Debe su nombre al salón de festejos, situado en el primer piso, que, en otros tiempos, se hallaba suntuosamente decorado con espejos venecianos. En el tímpano central entre las arcadas se encuentra el escudo de armas de su constructor, Federico II: el león palatino y los rombos bávaros y, en el tercer cuartel, la manzana imperial que le fué concedida por el emperador Carlos V en 1544 como símbolo de la dignidad de Mayordomo Mayor del Imperio.

La fachada de la construcción Ottheinrich está compuesta armónicamente por múltiples elementos y no hay otra como ella en los paises situados al norte de los Alpes. Fajas arquitectónicas artísticamente ornamentadas y semicolumnas de variada composición dividen la superficie de la fachada en tableros simétricos. Cada uno de ellos posee una bífora y una hornacina con figura decorativa. El Portal situado sobre la escalinata, profusamente articulado, se asemeja a un arco de triunfo y contiene, además de un medallón con la imagen de Ottheinrich, su escudo de armas y una inscripción. Frontones triangulares adornados con monedas romanas de la colección del constructor, siempre obsesionado por las artes, rematan las ventanas cruciformes de la planta baja. Junto a los atlantes del Portal podemos apreciar (de izquierda a derecha) las figuras de Josué, Sansón, Hércules y David – personajes heróicos del Antiguo Testamento. Una serie de figuras colocadas en el primer piso representan cinco de las virtudes: Fortaleza (con una columna destrozada), Fe (con la Biblia), Amor y Maternidad (con niños), Esperanza (con ancla) y la Justicia (con la balanza y la espada). Las siete figuras situadas en la parte superior representan dioses de la antigüedad romana – Saturno, Marte, Venus, Mercurio y Luna; encima, antiguamente delante de las dos casas de hastial, Sol y Jupiter – y corresponden al sol, la luna y los cinco grandes planetas. En la planta baja de la construcción Ottheinrich, en el edificio contiguo Ludwigbau y en la torre Apothekerturm (→ Torre de los farmacéuticos), el Museo Farmacéutico Alemán (→ Deutsches Apothekenmuseum) ha encontrado un alojamiento de estilo apropiado.

El escudo, con la fecha 1524 y situado en la torre escalonada central, alude a Luís V, el gran constructor del castillo. A continuación del ala antigua de su palacio residencial se encuentran las dependencias administrativas (→ Wirtschaftsgebäude), el patio de las fuentes (→ Brunnenhalle) y el edificio de los soldados (→ Soldatenbau) – hoy taquilla del castillo.

Distante del patio del castillo, y limitando con la terraza mirador – el Großer Altan (gran terrado) – se encuentra el edificio del tonel (→ Faßbau, la bodega), construído por Johann Kasimir (1583–1592). El pequeño terrado (→ Kleiner Altan) remata el edificio en su parte superior. En él se encuentra hoy el gigantesco tonel de Karl-Theodor que, con una cabida de 221 726 litros, es el mayor tonel del mundo. Está hecho de madera y puede llenarse. Para la construcción del recipiente (8,50 metros de largo por 7 metros de diámetro) se emplearon 130 robles. Su único adorno es el gran escudo de armas y las iniciales de Karl-Theodor. A la izquierda del compás y la garlopa – fueron empleados en su construcción – se encuentra todavía una parte de la cañería que, desde el tonel, llevaba el vino a la sala de festejos, el salón del rey, mediante la puesta en funcionamiento de una bomba elevadora. La pequeña estatua representa al diminuto Perkeo, bufón y vigilante del tonel en tiempos de Karl-Philipp y de Karl-Theodor. Según cuenta la leyenda, murió despues de haberse dejado persuadir para beber un vaso de agua en lugar del vino a que estaba acostumbrado. Todavía hoy es la figura simbólica del carnaval de Heidelberg. Las huellas que se encuentran en una de las losas de arenisca de la gran terraza son, según la leyenda, las de un caballero que, con toda la armadura y por ser repudiado por su amada, se arrojó desde la ventana de su aposento, situado en el piso más alto de la construcción Friedrichsbau.

Las fortificaciones del castillo

Ante un ataque del enemigo, la parte norte y oeste del castillo ofrecían muy poco peligro ya que la pendiente escarpada proporcionaba una defensa natural. Sin embargo, y precisamente en el extremo noroeste, encontramos la torre más consistente (30 metros de diámetro), la Dicker Turm (→ Torre Gruesa). Al ser volada, quedó en pie únicamente la parte exterior que da a la pendiente de la montaña ofreciendo un aspecto imponente de su fuerza defensiva en otros tiempos. Sus muros tenían un espesor de siete metros. En el siglo XVII mandó derribar el piso superior (la construcción de entramado primitiva) y en su lugar mandó construir – para ganar sitio – una sala de festejos y representaciones teatrales con grandes ventanales, pero de muy delgadas paredes, y de dieciséis esquinas. De esta forma consiguió un salón de baile, con una superficie de más de quinientos metros cuadrados, directamente junto a su residencia palaciega, el Englischer Bau (→ Construcción Inglesa).

La torre de la esquina noreste, la Glockenturm (→ campanario), fué en un principio simplemente un torreón de defensa de un piso. Con el tiempo se edificó sobre él una y otra vez y fué utilizado como vivienda.

Delante de la miranda (la gran terraza) fué instalada para la defensa del castillo la Gran Batería (→ Große Batterie). El príncipe elector Karl mandó reforzar el lado sudeste, en los años 1681–1683, con el fortín que lleva su nombre Karlsschanze y que está rematado por la torre artillera de cinco pisos. De esta fortificación, sin embargo, son pocos los restos de muralla que siguen en pie.

Los constructores de la fortificación utilizaron la ya mencionada Dicker Turm (→ Torre Gruesa) como eslabón entre el baluarte norte – debajo de la Construcción Inglesa – y el imponente baluarte oeste de Luís V. Aproximadamente en la parte central del flanco oeste, una torre provista de artillería, de gran espesor y semicircular – el Rondel –, formaba parte también de la fortificación. Un túnel comunicaba los sotanos del Rondel con la Torre Gruesa y continuaba, a través del baluarte norte, hasta el sotano de la construcción Friedrichsbau. Dos estatuas, semejantes a las de la construcción Friedrichsbau, representan a los príncipes electores Luís V y Federico V.

En 1619, Federico V mandó convertir el vallado en parque y tapar en parte el Rondel. El pequeño arco de triunfo, Elisabethentor (→ Arco de Isabel), es un regalo hecho a su esposa Elisabeth Stuart al cumplir los diecinueve años. Según la tradición fué instalado en una noche. Una placa conmemorativa, en la parte exterior del Stückgarten (→ Jardín de artillería), está dedicada a Johann W. Goethe, siete veces huesped en Heidelberg.

El enorme complejo defensivo del terraplén y el foso, situado en la parte oeste, lo mandó construir Luís V en sustitución de la antigua ronda que, al haberse edificado fuera de sus limites, se había hecho ineficaz. La pequeña torre fortificada situada en el angulo suroeste sirvió desde entonces como calabozo y se le dió el ingenioso nombre de «Seltenleer» (raramente vacante). En tiempos de paz, los señores palatinos utilizaban el foso para la cría de ciervos y, en tiempos de peligro, se llenaba con agua. La torre cuadrangular Torturm (→ Torre de acceso) fué la única que, por su forma, resistió los propósitos franceses de volarla. Dede la vaguada del foso del castillo, alcanza la respetable altura de cincuenta y dos metros. Su parte inferior era utilizada como mazmorra. Su entrada estaba protegida por cuatro puertas, un enorme rastrillo y un puente levadizo. Su única ornamentación son dos escuderos de piedra, toscamente labrados, y dos pequeños leones que soportaban el escudo de armas de los príncipes palatinos – probablemente de plata.

La muralla interior, situada en el ángulo sudeste entre la Torturm (→ Torre de acceso) y la imponente Pulverturm (→ Torre del polvorín), la mandó reforzar Luís V dándole un espesor de siete metros. La imponente torre Geschützturm (→ Torre de artillería), llamada también Krautturm («Kraut» → pólvora, Torre de la pólvora) ya que en el sótano de la misma se encontraba el polvorín, parece estar casi exclusivamente hecha de mampostería. Sea como fuere, sus paredes exteriores tienen un espesor de hasta seis metros y medio y un diámetro global de veinticuatro metros. Aguantó intacta los primeros intentos de voladura de los franceses en 1689; cuatro años más tarde, sin embargo, se vino abajo. Quedó fraccionada en dos y su parte exterior se desplomó sobre el foso del castillo. Ello permite ver el impresionante aspecto que ofrece el interior del coloso con sus tres departamentos de artillería superpuestos con sus bóvedas descansando sobre la pilastra central.

El lado este de castillo, y debido al corte profundo del valle (Friesental), poseía una defensa natural hasta que Federico V lo mandó tansformar en jardines en terraza de maravilloso trazado. La interceptada muralla y la ronda, situadas en el ángulo obtuso formado entre las torres Krautturm (→ Torre de la pólvora) y Glockenturm (→ campanario), están reforzadas además con una torre circular: la torre de los farmacéuticos (→ Apothekerturm). Hacia el año 1600, los propietarios del castillo construyeron en sustitución de la antigua ronda – desde los tiempos de Federico II, sobrepasada por las nuevas construcciones – una nueva, situada delante de las murallas exteriores y provista de una serie de cañones emplazados. Un adarve cubierto, situado en la parte sur del foso del castillo, aislaba del valle Friesental. La casamata triangular, situada delante de la torre de los farmacéuticos y construída despues de la Guerra de los Treinta Años, significó un nuevo refuerzo para el extenso flanco este.

La construcción del «Hortus Palatinus» (→ Jardín Palatino), sin embargo, y debido al terraplenaje de las cinco terrazas, supuso un sensible debilitamiento de esta posición defensiva. Para su construcción, Federico V ordenó levantar la vaguada veinte metros.

Obras de arquitectura religiosa

El centro del casco viejo de la ciudad es la imponente iglesia Heiliggeistkirche (→ Iglesia del Espíritu Santo). En 1400, el rey Ruperto el Palatino colocó la primera piedra de la actual iglesia de tres naves (central y colaterales). Este templo gótico, el mayor del antiguo Palatinado, era, a la vez, lugar dedicado a los oficios religiosos, sepultura de los miembros de la familia palatina y sala de festejos de la Universidad. El tejado actual y la cúpula, de estilo barroco, los mandó construir el príncipe elector Johan Wilhelm despues de las demoliciones sufridas durante la Guerra de Sucesión Palatina (1693). Sobre el portal central, situado en la parte de la Hauptstraße (→ Calle Mayor), encontramos tallados su escudo de armas y el de su esposa, de la familia de los Médicis.

En el interior de la iglesia llama la atención el gran contraste de luz entre el recinto coral (claro) y las naves (oscuras). Ello se debe a la posterior construcción de las galerías altas, destinadas a dar cabida a la voluminosa Biblioteca del Palatinado, la famosa «Bibliotheca Palatina». Mediante donaciones de la nobleza y de los príncipes electores – especialmente de Ottheinrich – y de Huldrich Fugger (Fúcar) – este último colaboró con doscientos treinta y cinco quintales de obras literarias – la «Bibliotheca Palatina» llegó a ser la mayor colección de libros de su tiempo. Despues de la toma de la ciudad por Tilly en 1623, el duque de Baviera Maximiliano se llevó – como botín de guerra, cargados en cincuenta carros – la más valiosa colección de Occidente, los libros de la biblioteca de la Universidad y los de la biblioteca privada de los príncipes electores y se los ofreció en donación al Vaticano. Solamente una pequeña parte de los mismos fué, más tarde, devuelta o rescatada. El salvajismo de los soldados del Rey Sol (en 1693) destruyó totalmente los monumentos funerarios de los príncipes electores. De los cincuenta y cinco sepulcros primitivos únicamente quedó intacto el del rey Ruperto el Palatino († 1410) y de su esposa.

La iglesia más antigua de Heidelberg fué la predecesora de la actual Iglesia de S. Pedro (→ Peterskirche), situada más arriba de la Plaza de la Universidad (→ Universitätsplatz). Por primera vez, y al ser construída la iglesia Heiliggeistkirche (Iglesia del Espíritu Santo, hacia el año 1400), Ruperto el Palatino la desvinculó de la pequeña Iglesia de S. Pedro y entregó ésta última a la Universidad. La actual construcción, de una sóla nave, fué edificada antes del año 1500. En ella se encuentran monumentos funerarios de profesores y ciudadanos insignes de los siglos XV al XIX.

La Iglesia de San Vito (→ St.-Vitus-Kirche), en Handschuhsheim, contiene importantes sepulturas del siglo XIV en adelante.

En el Heiligenberg (→ Monte Sacro), encima de Handschuhsheim, se hallan todavía los fundamentos del antiguo convento de San Miguel (→ Michaelskloster). Fué fundado en el año 870 por los monjes de Lorsch y está dedicado a «todos los santos».

Edificios públicos

Las tropas francesas se tomaron tan en serio su tarea destructora, en especial en el año 1693, que, en el ámbito del viejo Heidelberg, cási no quedó nada de las antiguas construcciones arquitectónicas. Quedó el arsenal (→ Zeughaus) – erróneamente llamado Marstall (→ Caballerizas), a orillas del río Néckar. Es utilizado como Mensa (comedor) para los estudiantes.

Inmediatamente después de la devastación de la ciudad, fué construída de nuevo, en la plaza que lleva su nombre, la vieja Universidad (→ Alte Universität). Posee una magnífica aula, decorada en estilo barroco. La histórica Studentenkarzer (cárcel de estudiantes), situada en la parte posterior del edificio, fué utilizada desde 1712 hasta 1914. En la parte posterior de la Nueva Universidad (→ Neue Universität), construída en 1931, quedó incluída la única que se conserva de la antigua muralla de la ciudad. Dado que por un tiempo fué utilizada como cárcel de mujeres, recibió el nombre de «Hexenturm» (→ Torre de las Brujas). La Biblioteca de la Universidad (→ Universitätsbibliothek, 1905), situada en lo alto del final de la calle Grabengasse (→ Calle del Foso), posee, junto a los manuscritos alemanes devueltos por el Vaticano, el famoso Manuscrito Manesse, rescatado de la biblioteca parisina en 1888.

La Plaza del Mercado (→ Marktplatz), sita entre la Iglesia Heiliggeist y el Ayuntamiento (→ Rathaus), construído hacia el año 1700 y de estilo barroco, era en la Edad Media centro de la vida social y lugar de las ejecuciones. Hay documentos que prueban que aquí, en 1525, «les fué cortada la cabeza a siete, y a tres los dedos».

La fuente del Kornmarkt (→ mercado del trigo), cási enfrente, está adornada con una estatua barroca de la Vírgen. Es una obra maestra de Peter van den Branden. Con la silueta del castillo al fondo, la «Kornmarktmadonna» (→ La Madonna del mercado del trigo) produce un efecto encantador.

Uno de los motivos más fotografiados en Heidelberg es el puente de Karl-Theodor (→ Karl-Theodor-Brücke), generalmente llamado Alte Brücke (→ Puente Viejo). Las torres son esencialmente todavía parte de la antigua fortificación medieval de la ciudad (siglo XIII). El actual puente de piedra fué construído por Karl-Theodor para sustituir el antiguo puente de madera cubierto que descansaba únicamente sobre pilastras de piedra y construído, en ambos extremos, como un puente levadizo. La torre oeste posee tres mazmorras, bajas y oscuras; la del este, una y la escalera de caracol. La estatua situada en el lado de la ciudad representa a Karl-Theodor, rodeado por las cuatro divinidades fluviales de sus patrimonios: Rín, Danubio, Néckar y Mosela. En el balcón de la parte norte, Minerva – diosa de la sabiduría y diosa protectora de castillos y ciudades – vela por la piedad, justicia, agricultura y comercio, por la astronomía, arquitectura, por la pintura y escultura, por la música. La estatua colocada en la cabecera norte del puente representa a San Juan Nepomuceno, santo bajo cuya invocación y protección se halla el puente.

Casas burguesas

Los soldados del «Rey Sol» Luís XIV de Francia ejecutaron la órden de destruir el Palatinado tan concienzudamente que, de la época anterior a 1693, únicamente quedó en pie la fachada de una casa burguesa: la del «Ritter» (→ Caballero), situada en la Hauptstraße (→ Calle Mayor) enfrente de la Iglesia Heiliggeistkirche.

El hugonote Charles Belier había mandado construir el suntuoso edificio en el año 1592 según el estilo renacentista. Una abundante ornamentación plástica embellece la fachada, especialmente los tableros salientes de los miradores de los pisos altos.

Despues de la total destrucción de la ciudad del año 1693, regresaron lentamente sus moradores a Heidelberg y levantaron de nuevo – la mayoría de las veces sobre los angostos fundamentos de las anteriores casas góticas – sencillas casas. De ésta forma se conservó intacto – en contra de los proyectos forjados por los príncipes electores – el plano general medieval. Algunos años más tarde, sin embargo, fueron edificados también edificios de mayor importancia como el Großherzogliches Palais (→ Palacio del Gran Duque, 1757), desde 1805 residencia en Heidelberg de los señores granducales de Báden, y el Palais Boisserée (→ Palacio de los hermanos Boisserée) en el que se hospedó Goethe en 1814 y 1815 en sus visitas a Heidelberg. También el Palais Morass – en la Hauptstraße, 97 – fué edificado en 1712 como elegante residencia señorial. Patio y jardín irradian todavía hoy una quietud contemplativa. Las piezas interiores, en parte adornadas con artísticos techos estucados, alojan la gran colección del Museo Palatino (→ Kurpfälzisches Museum).

Calles estrechas y angostas casas dominan la imagen de la parte oeste de la Heiliggeistkirche, de la calle Baja (→ Untere Straße) y sus calles laterales. En una de las calles laterales, en la Pfaffengasse (→ Calle de los Frailes), se encuentra la casa natal de Friedrich Ebert (→ Geburtshaus Friedrich Eberts), primer Presidente del Reich desde 1919 hasta 1925.

Quien con los ojos abiertos pasee por los callejones de los barrios viejos de Heidelberg, puede descubrir todavía simpaticos detalles: una escultura barroca en la hornacina de las casas, un escudo o uno de los muchos locales históricos. Heidelberg continúa siendo, pese a sus problemas de casas anticuadas y calles estrecheas, una ciudad en la que uno puede perder el corazón.

Heidelberg's Market Place showing Hercules' Well and the Town Hall (1701).
La place du Marché de Heidelberg avec la fontaine d'Hercule et l'hôtel de ville (1701).
La Plaza del Mercado de Heidelberg (→ Marktplatz) con la fuente de Hercules y el Ayuntamiento (→ Rathaus).

Hercules well in the market place.
La fontaine d'Hercule sur la place du marché.
La fuente de Hércules en la plaza del mercado.

Contemplative leisure time in the market place.
Moments contemplatifs sur la place du marché.
Momentos contemplativos en la plaza del mercado.

Market day at the foot of the Gothic Church of the Holy Ghost in the centre of the Old Town. ▷
Jour de marché aux pieds de l'église gothique du Saint-Esprit au centre de la vieille ville.
Día de mercado a los pies de la iglesia gótica Heiliggeistkirche en el centro del casco viejo de la ciudad.

The splendid Renaissance facade of Heidelberg's oldest burgher's house.

La magnifique façade Renaissance de la plus vieille maison bourgeoise de Heidelberg, le «Ritter».

Suntuosa fachada renacentista de la casa burguesa más antigua de Heidelberg: la casa del caballero (→ Ritter).

A typical narrow lane in the old part of the city: «Die Untere Strasse».
Une ruelle typique de la vieille ville: «Die Untere Straße» (Rue inférieure).
Típica callejuela de la parte antigua del ciudad: «Die Untere Straße».

A popular conveyance.
Un moyen de transport très populaire.
El medio de transporte popular.

Small shops at the Heiliggeistkirche [Church of the Holy Ghost].
Petites échoppes accolées à l'église du Saint-Esprit.
Tiendecitas junto a la iglesia Heiliggeistkirche.

The «Old University», the oldest building of the «Rupert Carola».

La «vieille université», le plus vieux bâtiment de l'université «Ruperta Carola».

La vieja Universidad (→ «Alte Universität»), es el edificio más antiguo de la Universidad «Ruperta Carola».

The principal lecture theatre «Aula» of the Old University which was ▷ restored in 1886 on the occasion of the University's fifth centenary.

La grande salle des fêtes de la Vieille Université restaurée en 1886 à l'occasion des festivités du 500ᵉ anniversaire.

El Aula de la «Vieja Universidad», renovada con ocasión de su quinto Centenario.

The «Mensur»: scene from student life.
La mensur: scène de la vie estudiantine.
Duelo entre estudiantes: escena de la vida estudiantil.

Student life in the «Zum Ochsen» Inn.
Vie estudiantine dans l'auberge «Zum Roten Ochsen» (Au Boeuf rouge).
Vida de los estudiantes en la fonda Gasthaus zum Ochsen.

Cell in the Students' prison.
Cellule du cachot des étudiants.
Celda de arresto en Studentenkarzer (cárcel de estudiantes).

Wall painting of students under arrest in the Students' Jail.
Dessins et graffitis des détenus du cachot des étudiants.
Frescos pintados por arrestados en la cárcel de estudiantes (→ Studentenkarzer). ▷

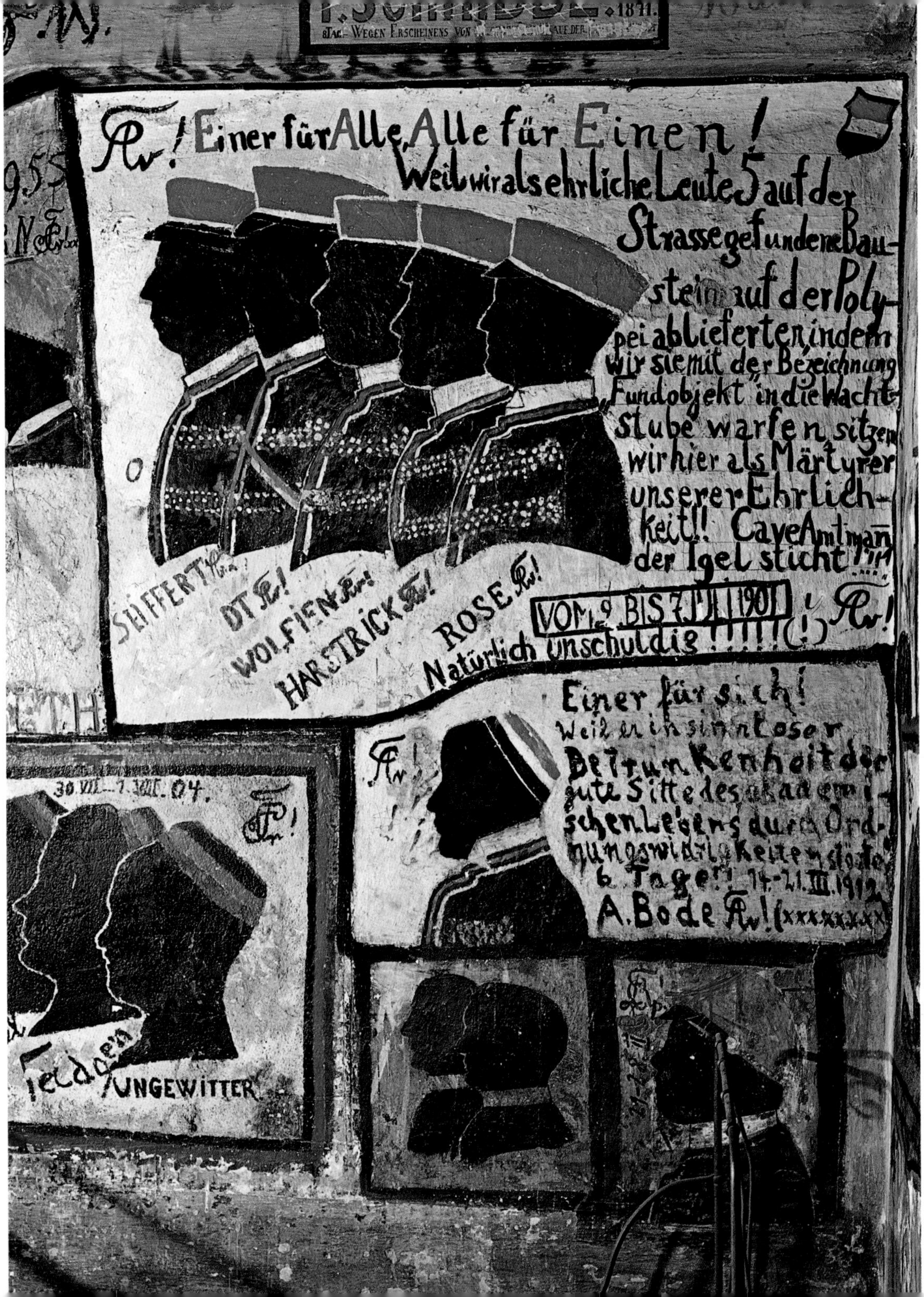

I. SCHNABEL 1871
Ga:- WEGEN ERSCHEINENS VON ... AUE DER

Aw! Einer für Alle Alle für Einen!

Weil wir als ehrliche Leute 5 auf der Strasse gefundene Bau-stein auf der Poly-pei ablieferten, indem wir sie mit der Bezeichnung "Fundobjekt" in die Wacht-stube warfen, sitzen wir hier als Märtyrer unserer Ehrlich-keit!! Cave Amtman der Igel sticht!

SHIFFERT DT! WOLFIEN HARSTRICK ROSE Aw! Natürlich unschuldig!!!!! (!) Aw!

VOM 9 BIS 7.II 1901

Einer für sich! Weil er in sinnloser Betrunkenheit die gute Sitte des akademi-schen Lebens durch Ord-nungswidrigkeiten tötete 6 Tage! 14-21.III.1912 A.Bode Aw! (xxxxxxxx

30.VII—1.VIII.04.

Felden UNGEWITTER

The Bronze Ape near the Old Bridge Gate holds his mirror up to his observers.
La porte du Pont, un singe de bronze tient un miroir pour les passants.
El mono de bronce del «Brückentor» muestra el espejo a su observador.

View through the Bridge Gate into the Steingasse (stone lane) with the ▷
Church of the Holy Spirit in the background.
Vue à travers la porte du pont sur la Steingasse (ruelle pavée), avec l'église du
Saint-Esprit en arrière-plan.
La iglesia Heiliggeistkirche a través del portal del puente y la Steingasse.

The Palais Boisserée at the Karlsplatz
Le palais Boisserée sur la place Karl.
El Palais Boisserée junto a la plaza Karlsplatz.

View over the Corn Market to the castle ruins.
Vue du Kornmarkt sur les ruines du château (Marché au grain).
Panorámica del Kornmarkt sobre la ruina del castillo.

The sign «Zum Roten Ochsen».
Enseigne «Zum Roten Ochsen».
Rótulo «Zum Roten Ochsen».

Brisk activity in the pedestrian precinct.
Grande animation dans la zone piétonne.
Animado trajín en la zona peatonal.

The Altar of the Twelve Apostles, carved by Riemenschneider and now in the Kurpfalz Museum.

Le retable des Douze Apôtres de Riemenschneider exposé au musée du Palatinat électoral.

Altar de los 12 Apóstoles de Riemenschneider; se encuentra en el Museo Palatino.

Kurfürst Ottheinrich (1556–1559), creator of the most splendid of castle palaces in Heidelberg.

L'Electeur Othon-Henri (1556–1559), bâtisseur du plus somptueux des palais du château.

Ottheinrich (1556–1559), principe elector y creador del más suntuoso palacio del castillo.

Heidelberg's most famous promenade, Philosopher's Way.
La plus fameuse promenade de Heidelberg, surnommée le chemin des Philosophes.
El lugar de paseo más famoso de Heidelberg, el camino de los filósofos (→ Philosophenweg).

The Old Bridge and Castle seen in front of Königstuhl's heights.
Vieux-Pont et château de Heidelbeg; au fond, le «Königstuhl», ou Trône du roi.
Viejo Puente y Castillo. Al fondo, la montaña de Heidelberg: Königstuhl. ▷

◁ *View of the old bridge and the Heiliggeistkirche [Church of the Holy Ghost].*
Vue sur le vieux pont et l'église du Saint-Esprit.
Panorámica sobre el antiguo puente y la iglesia Heiliggeistkriche.

Old Bridge showing statue of Athene.
Le Vieux-Pont et la statue de Pallas Athénée.
El Viejo Puente con la estatua de Minerva.

◁ *Gate of the Old Bridge, right, statue of its builder, Karl Theodor.*
La porte du Vieux-Pont et, à droite, la statue de son bâtisseur, Charles-Théodore.
El portal del Viejo Puente; a la derecha, una estatua de su fundador: Karl-Theodor.

Bismarck Square. The centre point for local traffic.
La place Bismarck. Le noeud de communication des transports en commun locaux.
Bismarckplatz, la plaza de Bismarck. El centro de la red de comunicaciones local.

Theodor-Heuss Bridge.
Le pont Theodor-Heuss.
El puente Theodor-Heuss-Brücke.

◁ *Evening romance at the Old Bridge.*
Impressions romanesques au Vieux Pont.
Ambiente romántico por la tarde sobre el Viejo Puente.

Neckar bank in the spring.
Les berges du Neckar au printemps.
Orilla del Neckar en primavera.

View from Philosopher's Way.
Vue depuis le chemin des Philosophes.
Desde el «Philosophenweg»: Vista de la ciudad.

Castle illuminations and fireworks.
Illumination du château avec feux d'artifice.
Iluminación del castillo con sus fuegos artificiales.

View of Heidelberg and the expanses of the Rhine plain from the viewing platform of the television tower.

Coup d'œuil de la plate-forme avec beau point de vue de la tour de télévision sur Heidelberg et les vastes espaces de la plaine du Rhin.

Vista desde el mirador de la torre de televisión sobre Heidelberg y la vastedad de la Uanura del Rin.

The Königstuhl. ▷
Le Königstuhl.
En el monte Konigstuhl.

The Königstuhl.
Le Königstuhl.
En el monte Königstuhl.

The old mountain railway on the summit of Königstuhl.
Le vieux funiculaire au sommet du Königstuhl.
Antiguo ferrocarril de montaña en la cima del Königstuhl.

View of Heidelberg from across the Neckar valley.
Vue de la vallée du Neckar sur Heidelberg.
Panorámica del valle del Neckar sobre la ciudad de Heidelberg.

View of Neckargemünd.
Vue sur Neckargemünd.
Panorámica sobre Neckargemünd.

The Parish Church of Neckarsteinach.
L'église paroissiale de Neckarsteinach.
La iglesia parroquial de Neckarsteinach.

The little town of Hirschhorn on the German fortress road.
La petite ville de Hirschhorn sur la route allemande des châteaux-forts.
La pequeña ciudad Hirschhorn junto a la carretera alemana de los castillos (Burgenstraße).

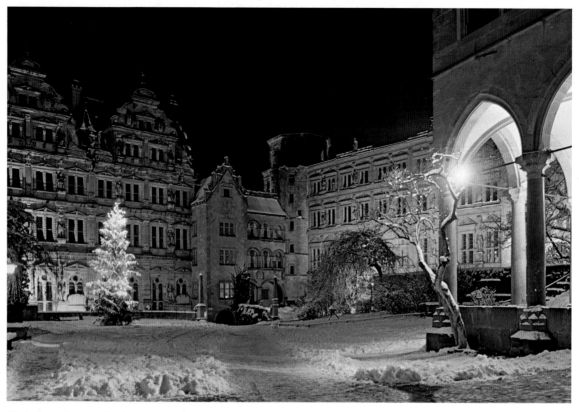

Christmas in the Castle courtyard.
Noël dans la cour du château.
Navidad en el patio del castillo.

◁ *The peace of evening over Heidelberg.*
Heidelberg à la tombée de la nuit.
Ambiente vespertino de la ciudad.

Winter in the castle gardens. ▷
Le jardin du château en hiver.
Los jardines del castillo en invierno.

Winter idyll at the Old Bridge.
Tableau idyllique d'hiver au Vieux Pont.
Idilio de invierno sobre el Viejo Puente.